AN INTRODUCTION TO
Wild Flowers

by
JOHN KIERAN

Illustrations by Tabea Hofmann

Doubleday & Company, Inc.

Garden City, New York

INDEX

Library of Congress Catalog Card Number 65-17931
Copyright © 1965 by John Kieran

Copyright, 1948, 1952,

Printed in the United States of America.

by Doubleday & Company, Inc.

TYPOGRAPHY BY JAMES LEACH
9 8 7 6 5 4

ISBN: 0-385-04549-2

FOREWORD

In the Bible we find the words: "Consider the lilies of the field, how they grow; they toil not, neither do they spin; yet...Solomon in all his glory was not arrayed as one of these." A wonderful observation. We live in a flowering world and should make the most of it. On an ordinary ramble through the fields and woods at the proper season, anyone who knows and loves wild flowers will find beauty beyond price and have hours of enjoyment at no cost. The difficulty lies in getting started.

It seems logical to follow *An Introduction to Birds* with this *Introduction to Wild Flowers*. You can't go looking for birds without finding flowers, particularly in the high tide of the Spring migration. Like its companion work, this is a book for beginners of all ages. Flowers are a delight in childhood and a source of continued enjoyment in later years. What will come as a pleasant surprise to novices in the field is the abundance and infinite variety of the flowering plants that grow in any area and that can be enjoyed through most of the months of the year. In fact, there are so many that the beginner might recoil in dismay if handed a volume containing a scientific survey of the flowering plants of even a small section of the country.

Here we take the easy painless way to acquire a step-by-step acquaintance with some of the more common wild flowers of our woods and fields, our swamps and roadsides, our hills and hollows. Once that much is attained, the beginner can go on to a wider knowledge and a deeper appreciation of the beauties and marvels of the plant world. For the advanced student, the botanist presents Orders, Families, Genera and Species in systematic sequence for which there is rule and reason. But this is a primer. Here we present only a hundred common flowers that the beginner might find simply by going outdoors and keeping his or her eyes open.

It's true that some—perhaps too many—of the "common wild flowers" included in this book are common largely in the northeastern section of the United States and less common or perhaps even missing in other regions. That's because of my limited excursions as a traveling botanist. The flowers that I look upon as common are the wild flowers that flourish in the fields and forests of New York and New England, which are my "home ground," the territory that I have roamed at all seasons and in every kind of weather since I was a boy. Those that are presented in this book are arranged approximately in the order in which you will find them coming into bloom if you start looking "when the hounds of Spring are on Winter's traces" and continue your search through the warm days of Summer to the killing frosts of oncoming Winter.

One rule holds true about trying to learn something about birds and flowers; to get to know them you must look not only for them but at them! At first glance it's easy to overlook significant details. So look closely and keenly and when you think you have noted everything of importance, look again. I know how much may be missed by lack of observation, because in my early days afield I found that somehow I often overlooked things that were right under my nose, so to speak. It's astonishing how much more you see when you take a second look—or a third.

The differences between birds and flowers are many, and so are the methods by which the beginner may learn something about either or both. For one thing, flowers do not sing or call to one another. You can't track them down by the sounds they utter or identify them by ear without seeing them. On the other hand, flowers are not flighty. They are not here one second and gone the next. If you see a flower at all, it will hold still while you inspect it. If somebody tells you where to find a clump of Trailing Arbutus in redolent bloom in May, you can march right to the spot with perfect confidence that the little cream-colored chalices—and the delightful perfume—will be waiting for you. But the Magnolia Warbler that your informant saw overhead at the same spot may be miles away when you arrive.

In fairness to the birds, however, it must be admitted that some species like the Chickadee, the White-breasted Nuthatch, the Downy Woodpecker and the Crow are around all year wearing the same costumes for easy identification, whereas most flowers have a limited blooming period during which beginners may find them and recognize them. There are advantages on both sides, but it seems to me that the searcher for wild flowers has an easier task that can be approached with greater assurance. If you "know a bank whereon the wild thyme blows, where oxlips and the nodding violet grows," the chances are that you will find them there year after year and from dawn to dark during the blooming period. You can't trust any bird to hold still for an hour.

One of the things that a beginner will soon learn is that flowers come in strange forms and what look for all the world like petals may be something else—bracts, sepals, parts of leaves or even whole flowers in themselves. Once you begin to take an interest in the subject and read even as simple a book as this about wild flowers, you will be astonished at some of your discoveries. I will not anticipate them here, because that would be taking some of the fun out of it. There is always an added thrill in finding out something for yourself. I have tried to make the text as helpful as possible in guiding the beginner to an understanding of what actually constitutes the "flower" of what a botanist would describe as a "flowering plant."

On the technical side I have abided by Gray's *Manual of Botany* (Eighth or Fernald Edition) for botanical details and scientific names. Beyond that I am deeply indebted to the late Dr. Edgar T. Wherry, formerly of the University of Pennsylvania, for aid and comfort in preparing this book and for his critical reading of the manuscript. The writing has been a labor of love for me but it has kept me long hours at a desk. Now that I have finished I can go out again in search of wild flowers, a pursuit of which I never tire, particularly at this time of year when—in the wonderful words of Swinburne—

> *Winter's rains and ruins are over*
>
>   .   .   .   .
>
> *And time remembered is grief forgotten,*
> *And frosts are slain and flowers begotten,*
> *And in green underwood and cover,*
>   *Blossom by blossom the Spring begins.*

John Kieran

May, 1963

SKUNK CABBAGE
(*Symplocarpus foetidus*)

The lowly Skunk Cabbage deserves honorable mention if for no other reason than that in the swamps, low meadows, and wet woods, it is the herald of Spring over a large section of North America, the first wild flowering plant to thrust itself above the ground and burst into bloom. It's true that its flowers are not spectacular in size or color. In fact, you have to get down on your hands and knees to see the flowers at all. If you lower yourself to that extent and peer inside the heavy, twisting, purple-streaked helmet or hood by which we all recognize the plant, you will see a thick stalk on which there is something like an egg-shaped, brownish-yellow pincushion. The many and somewhat raggedy "eruptions" on that pincushion are the true flowers of the Skunk Cabbage.

Botanists call the helmet or hood a "spathe" and the flowering stalk a "spadix" in the Skunk Cabbage, the Jack-in-the-pulpit, and other plants that flower in the same fashion. The "skunk" part of the name comes from the disagreeable odor given off by the Skunk Cabbage when crushed, and the "cabbage" part is a tribute to the large cabbage-like leaves that come after the flowering period and flourish mightily in moist places throughout the Summer. The helmets of the early Spring rarely exceed 6 inches in height but the broad leaves may stretch up 2 feet or more. The Skunk Cabbage is found from Nova Scotia to Georgia and as far west as Minnesota and Iowa. The Western Skunk Cabbage, common along the Pacific Coast, differs from this species in having a bright yellow, shell-like spathe.

Don't look down upon the Skunk Cabbage because of its low estate, its soggy surroundings, and its lack of bright colors. Much can be learned from this sturdy plant that shoulders its way up through frosted ground and often blooms defiantly in the snow when "Winter, lingering, chills the lap of Spring." From the Skunk Cabbage we can learn that some plants flower before they produce leaves, and that flowers may be small, comparatively colorless, and located in odd places on a plant. We could learn many other things from the Skunk Cabbage, but perhaps the first lesson is best closed with a few words from the diary of Henry David Thoreau, whose keen eye noticed that the Skunk Cabbages in a swamp near his Concord home never completely surrendered to oncoming Winter. Even as the broad leaves withered and fell under the impact of Autumn he noticed the hoods beginning to form for the Spring push. And so he wrote of them: "They see over the brow of Winter's hill. They see another Summer ahead."

[9]

COLTSFOOT
(*Tussilago farfara*)

This low-growing, bright yellow flower of the early Spring is common only in the northeastern section of the United States, and even there it often goes unnoticed because, at a casual glance, it is easily mistaken for a Dandelion. A closer look will show that the Coltsfoot bloom is smaller and the flower stalk—the "scape" of the botanist—is not smooth and hollow as in the Dandelion but quite hairy and made up of overlapping segments. The leaves, coming after the flowers have gone to seed, are supposed to be about the size and shape of a colt's foot—hence the name—but the outline is jagged all the way around. The plant was brought from Europe by early colonists on the theory that its juices would cure colds, and for generations many country stores in New England sold Coltsfoot candy sticks that children liked well enough because there was more sugar in them than Coltsfoot flavor. The plant grows on sterile, gravelly, or muddy slopes, roadside embankments and such places. It has lost standing as a cold cure but is gaining ground steadily as the wind carries its plumed seeds to new locations.

DANDELION
(*Taraxacum officinale*)

This must be the best-known flower in the world, and one of the most unappreciated. It is found in all inhabited regions of the earth. Where men can live the Dandelion will lift its golden head through most months of the year, but, because it is so widespread and so abundant, its beauty is overlooked. The plant has

another good point. Dandelion salad is a regular part of the food supply of families in many countries. The narrow leaves with the jagged edges gave the plant the French name of "*Dent-de-lion*," or "lion's tooth," centuries ago, and we have taken over the name in slightly changed form. Owners of well-kept lawns usually look upon Dandelions as impudent intruders and go after them with vigor and indignation, but children still view the bright yellow flower head with high favor. It catches their youthful eyes and they are allowed to pick it unhindered. And what fun at a later stage when the flower head has become a feathery sphere and they blow on it in a childish attempt to know "what o'clock" it may be! There is much to be said for the humble, abundant, and beautiful Dandelion.

HEPATICA
(*Hepatica americana*)

Over a large section of North America—from Florida to Nova Scotia, from Missouri to Manitoba—the first flower of Spring to appear in the upland woods is the Hepatica, called Liverleaf or Liverwort in some regions because its 3-lobed leaves are somewhat liver-shaped in general outline. Indeed, the name Hepatica is derived from the Greek "*hepar*," meaning liver, there being an ancient belief that the plant could cure diseases of this organ. From among the dead leaves of the forest floor the fuzzy flower stalks—"scapes" technically—push up to a height of 3 to 6 inches, each bearing a single flower about ½-inch in diameter and usually pale blue, but it may be light purple, pink, or even white. There may be from 6 to 12 or more "petals" that are really sepals but we need not get excited about the difference. There are many flowers whose sepals look like petals to the ordinary eye. Of these the botanists write: "Sepals, petaloid." At the time of flowering, only last year's Hepatica leaves—thick, fleshy, and rusty green—are found at the base of the flowering stalks. The new leaves come later and lie along or hang just above the litter of the forest floor.

DUTCHMAN'S-BREECHES
(*Dicentra cucullaria*)

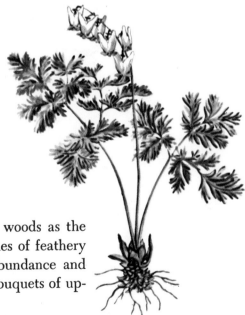

The name, the shape, and the general appearance of this flower combine to make it a favorite with children wherever it grows, and it is found over most of North America east of the Rockies and also in the Pacific Northwest. It seems like something that might be produced in a toy shop or sold at a candy counter. The flower stalks with their 4 to 12 "little breeches" hanging from them are from 5 to 10 inches tall. The lacy leaves, cut into innumerable feathery green ribbons, are almost as attractive as the flowers. The leaves come up first in the Spring. Look for patches of them on slopes and in glens in rich woods as the snow disappears. A little later these green patches of feathery foliage will produce Dutchman's-breeches in abundance and give children the chance to pick their first real bouquets of upland flowers of the season.

BLOODROOT
(*Sanguinaria canadensis*)

There is no more beautiful or delicate flower in the wildwood than the angelic-looking Bloodroot that is found in early Spring in rich woods over most of North America east of the Rocky Mountains. This plant likes moist banks and shelves in rocky woods. The flowers are found in clumps, groups, and patches, springing up from rootstocks that run under the forest floor. Despite the fact that the flower is pure white, strikingly lovely, and fairly common over such a wide territory, it is not always easy to find. For one thing, it doesn't grow just everywhere in the woods but only in favorable locations to which it is faithful. Another thing is that leaf and flower come up quickly together and a thick, fleshy, and deeply lobed leaf usually curves in cylinder fashion around the rising flower stem—"scape" to the botanist—as though to protect the bud from the bitter winds or the cold rains of the early season. When you find the Bloodroot you will notice that the leaf and flower stalks part company where they come out of the ground but, nevertheless, they grow up in close contact to a height of 8 to 16 inches, and the bud generally overtops the leaf at the last.

But even when the buds burst open and the 6 to 16 petals of each flower form themselves into a wonderful white chalice, you have to be alert to find them because they come and go so fast. If you want to see Bloodroot at its peak, you have to be as regular as a watchman making his rounds. If you miss even a few days of patrol, the glory may have departed from the Bloodroot of your territory. The best way to find the flower is to look for the leaves curved protectively around the flower stalk as they come up from the ground. These leaves are so thick and tender to the touch that they seem to be made out of something like gray-green rubber. But their size and odd appearance catch the eye, and it is easy to find them if you patrol suitable locations faithfully at the right time—which varies from late March to May, depending upon where you live. When the flower bud rises above the leaf the time of blooming is at hand and will pass quickly. Be vigilant!

The unlovely name—Bloodroot—for such a lovely flower is due to the crimson juice that comes from any break in the plant, particularly the rootstock. The scientific name *Sanguinaria* is a reference to the same peculiarity, being derived from the Latin word for blood. It is said that the American Indians used a dye made from the red juice of this plant not only in coloring their garments and handiwork but also as a war paint when occasion called for such decoration.

MARSH MARIGOLD
(*Caltha palustris*)

These are the bright golden flowers of the wet meadows, brooksides, and swamplands that country folk often call "Cowslips" and which some of them use as the first "greens" or "pot-herbs" of the season, eating buds, young leaves, stems, and all. They gather it, treat it, cook it, and eat it much as they do spinach. The plant stem is thick, fleshy, and hollow, and the leaves are large and round. The flower-bearing stalks may carry the blooms to a height of 1 or 2 feet above the ground. Here again the glowing yellow "petals"—there may be from 5 to 9 of them—are really sepals. If you look underneath these golden offerings you will see that they do not have the usual green sepals that are found under the colored petals of many flowers. In this case— as in some other flower families—the petals are missing and the sepals, turning to a glistening gold color, look just as bright as any petals could be in the Spring sunlight.

This is a plant that loves to "keep its feet wet" without going overboard. It is found from Newfoundland to Alaska and as far south as Nebraska and the Carolinas. It comes into bloom in late March in the southerly part of its range and may be found in flower in June in its northerly homelands. It looks something like a stout Buttercup and, indeed, is a member of the large Crowfoot Family along with the Buttercup, Hepatica, Anemone, Columbine, and Pasque Flower. The explanation of its scientific name, *Caltha palustris*, is that "*caltha*" is the Latin name for Marigold and "*palustris*" is Latin for "swampy," referring to the fact that the Marsh Marigold prefers wet ground generally and flourishes abundantly in swamps.

There are days in Spring before the Alders, Dogwoods, Viburnums, Willows, and Red Maples have spread their greenery when such swamps seem to be floored with gold, so thickly spread and so sturdily displayed are the bright yellow flowers of this plant. Later the same area will be the "haunt of coot and hern," the home of the Red-winged Blackbird, the lurking place of the Yellowthroat, the feeding ground of the Bittern, the concert stage of the Veery—or the Willow Thrush of the Northwest. It is a good thing to keep such matters in mind, because it is impossible to go looking for flowers without finding birds, just as it is impossible to go looking for birds without finding flowers—and shrubs and trees and insects and other things, too. One thing leads to another outdoors. Nothing stands alone or lives alone. And nowhere better than in a swamp is this community of interests so well established and so easily observed. Most persons look on swamps as waste territory but to lovers of wildlife they are happy hunting grounds.

[13]

SPRING BEAUTY
(*Claytonia virginica*)

To be specific, this is the Narrow-leaved Spring Beauty that carpets the Spring woods from Quebec to Georgia and from Minnesota to Texas. It's a plant from 4 to 7 inches in height with grasslike leaves and anywhere from 2 to 40 flowering stems that carry loose clusters—"racemes," the botanists call these clusters—of white flowers with pink veins or pinkish flowers with darker veins. The flowers are 5-petaled and when fully open may measure 1 inch across, but they close up tight in cold snaps or even when the sky is overcast on cool days. You may find the woodland floor almost white with them one day, and the next day, if it has turned cold, you will have to look close to find any trace of the whiteness so conspicuous the previous day. There are close relatives of the Narrow-leaved Spring Beauty in other parts of the country, all differing a bit in leaf and flower, but if you know this one—and it is easy to find and identify—you will recognize the others as relatives. The Latin name of the group, *Claytonia*, is a memorial to Dr. John Clayton, a colonial botanist who was born in England but spent most of his life—he died in 1773—in Virginia.

TRAILING ARBUTUS
(*Epigaea repens*)

There is no difficulty in recognizing the lowly, lovely, and fragrant Trailing Arbutus; the trick is to find it. Though it ranges all the way from Newfoundland to Saskatchewan and south to Florida and Mississippi, it is rarely abundant in any locality. It likes shady places and most often is found in clumps and patches in the woods, particularly where there are evergreens. But it may be found in shaded nooks in old pastures too. It is called the Mayflower in many regions—particularly New England—but so many other flowers are also called Mayflowers that it is better to call this one the Trailing Arbutus. It really does trail along the ground on hairy stems and twigs, bearing its thick, oval, green and often rusty leaves and, in April or May, its clusters of little tubed pinkish flowers whose 5-lobed "faces" are about ½-inch in diameter. The flowers are waxy but sturdy and stand up well through late frosts and cold rains of unsettled Spring weather. When you come upon a clump of Trailing Arbutus, get on your hands and knees and inhale the wonderful perfume for which the flower is famed. But do not pick the flowers. They are too lovely; they are too scarce; they are too valuable. This is so well recognized that in many regions it is unlawful to pick them. But it is not against the law to look for them, find them, and enjoy their fragrance.

PASQUE FLOWER
(*Anemone patens*)

This is the hairy-stemmed, golden-centered, pale purple or pinkish-blue flower that covers the open hillsides, the great plains, and the wide prairies from Illinois to Texas and north to British Columbia in early Spring. In addition to Pasque Flower, it is called Prairie Smoke, Wild Crocus, Rock Lily, Hartshorn Plant, Headache Plant, and probably many other things in different sections in which it flourishes. The leaves that branch off from the base of the stem are cut and slashed into numerous ribbon-like segments, and the woolly stem may carry its single flower to a height of from 1 to 1½ feet. The color of the flower varies from purple to almost pure white, and the blooming period extends from March in the southerly part of its range to May in the northerly area. Though it will make no difference to beginners in the field—meaning the readers of this book—the 5 to 7 "petals" around the golden center of the Pasque Flower are not petals but colorful sepals. It's a trait of the Anemones to display sepals instead of petals and the Latin name of the Pasque Flower shows that it is one of the Anemones.

However, there is no other native Anemone that puts on such a magnificent display over such a wide area. It is so popular in South Dakota that it has been named the State flower there, and it is a prime favorite with children all over its range. There are more or less good reasons for some of the names by which this flower is known. It is called Pasque Flower because it blooms about Easter time over much of its range and Easter is the Pasque or Paschal Feast on the church calendar. It is called Wild Crocus because it pushes up quickly from the bare ground in early Spring like the cultivated Crocus and also bears some resemblance to the Crocus in shape and color. It is called Prairie Smoke in parts of its range because, after the blooming period, the golden center of the flower becomes a globular mass of silky hairs like the Dandelion head in the "five o'clock" stage—the ripening seeds with feathery attachments—and when the wind blows these feathery masses about, the effect is that of low waves of smoke moving across the prairies. The feathery appendages, of course, help in the distribution of the seeds by the wind. Many plants use that method of seed distribution, but there are some that use running water, flying birds, or ambling animals to spread their seeds around. Some even shoot their seeds out as from spring-guns! The variety and ingenuity of these methods are amazing. You can learn more by watching flowers go to seed than by looking at them in bloom.

WINDFLOWER
(*Anemone quinquefolia*)

With thin stems and light leaves that tremble at every whisper of the wind, these dainty little white flowers are well-named. In fact, the scientific name traces back to "*anemos,*" the Greek word for "wind." There are in North America about 20 species of Anemone, differing in size and color as well as shape of leaves. The Windflower, also called the Wood Anemone, is found in open woods, thickets, and clearings from Quebec to Manitoba and Minnesota, and southward as far as North Carolina and Kentucky. It grows to a height of from 4 to 9 inches with 3 leaves, each divided into 5 parts with rather pointed ends, at a wide angle on the stem several inches or more below the single flower with 4 to 10 white "petaloid sepals" that look like petals to the ordinary eye. Much of what is said about the Windflower is also true of the Rue Anemone, a near relative and a fellow member of the great Crowfoot Family. The Rue Anemone is about the same size and color as the Windflower and grows in the same places over much of the Windflower range, but the Rue Anemone leaves are gently lobed or "scalloped," there are two or more flowers at the top of the stem and usually a "collarette" of leaflets just beneath the flowers.

BLUETS; QUAKER LADIES; HOUSTONIA
(*Houstonia caerulea*)

This dainty little light blue flower is found underfoot in open grassy places as soon as Spring really warms to its work. It is common in New England and as far south as Georgia, but it thins out to the westward and a traveler would be hard put to find a goodly clump of it in most of the country west of the Mississippi. It is a little plant quite

grasslike in appearance that grows to a height of from 3 to 7 inches with the small pale blue flowers with lighter centers—usually white with a touch of yellow —trembling shyly at the touch of every passing breeze. The petals are joined in a tube that opens into 4 divisions in a flower "face" that is about ⅜-inch across. Sometimes they are numerous enough to seem like a blue haze running through the grass in all directions. They love pasture lands. In addition to Bluets, Quaker Ladies, and Houstonia, they are also called Innocence, Eyebright, Nuns, Little Washerwomen, and Quaker Bonnets. If you are in doubt about the local name, ask the neighbors.

[16]

VIRGINIA BLUEBELL; VIRGINIA COWSLIP
(*Mertensia virginica*)

This plant—the Mertensia of the cultivated gardens—has crossed the Canadian Border in a few favored places, but mostly it is found in wet meadows, around the edges of marshes, and along the banks of streams across the United States from the Atlantic Coast region to the Rocky Mountains. It's smooth and fleshy in leaf and stalk, with oval leaves from 2 to 5 inches long, the upper ones smaller and "sessile" or "sitting on the main stem" that rises to a height of 1 to 2 feet or possibly a little higher. The numerous flowers are carried at the top in what are called "terminal" clusters. Occasionally the main stem has branches and in such cases there are flower clusters at the ends of these, too. The flowers are narrowly bell-shaped, or perhaps you might call them trumpet-shaped, about 1 inch long, with the flaring open ends rather gently 5-sided. The buds are pink, but the color of the open flowers varies from pinkish-purple to lavender-blue. Sometimes the flowers are almost white, but in general they display the hue that justifies the name "Bluebells" by which they are known over much of their range.

Another name for this plant is Lungwort, derived from an ancient belief that some part of it—whether leaf, flower, stalk, or root is not stated—would cure diseases of the

lungs. The ending "wort" is frequently found in flower names such as Liverwort (Hepatica), St. John's-wort, Miterwort, Ragwort, Spiderwort, the Figworts, and many more. The "wort" part comes from the old Anglo-Saxon "wyrt," which simply means "plant." Thus Liverwort is supposed to be good for diseases of the liver, Lungwort is credited with being helpful in cases of lung trouble, and Frances Theodora Parsons wrote of St. John's-wort that "it was formerly gathered on St. John's Eve and was hung at the doors and windows as a safeguard against thunder and evil spirits." In olden days the magical properties of plants were taken quite seriously by many of the populace but now they survive only as quaint legend.

One way in which botanists may do honor to their friends is to name plants after them. Thus the scientific name of the Virginia Bluebell is *Mertensia virginica*, the second part of which does honor to Virginia where presumably the species was first found and the first part is in memory of Franz Karl Mertens, a German botanist who lived from 1764 to 1831 and will never be completely forgotten as long as the *Mertensia* comes into bloom.

[17]

TROUT LILY; DOG'S-TOOTH VIOLET
(*Erythronium americanum*)

In moist woods and thickets and the more solid parts of shady bogs you will find the mottled leaves of this beautiful low-growing flower carpeting the ground soon after the snow has departed. The smooth flower stem rises to a height of 6 to 10 inches from between the two narrow mottled leaves that point in opposite directions. The single nodding yellow flower has 6 segments that curl back at the tips when in full bloom. This species—there are more than a dozen close relatives in different parts of the country—is found from Nova Scotia across Canada to western Ontario and in the United States from Maine to Florida and as far west as Minnesota and Oklahoma. Dog's-tooth Violet is a poor name for this flower. It is not a member of the Violet family and doesn't look like a dog's tooth. Some call it Adder's-tongue because of a fancied resemblance of the stamens to a snake's tongue. But John Burroughs, the famous naturalist, gave it the name Trout Lily because it is a member of the Lily Family and comes into bloom at the start of the trout season. Fawn Lily is another name, appropriate because of its dappled leaves.

LARGE-FLOWERED BELLWORT; GREAT MERRYBELLS
(*Uvularia grandiflora*)

The pale yellow Bellworts or Merrybells flourish in close company in rich woods, and the plants hang their heads as though they had done something of which they were all ashamed. They are from 10 to 20 inches in height, and, with narrow drooping leaves partially concealing the downcast flowers, they look like miniature patches of sowed corn in the woodlands. They are found from Nova Scotia to Georgia and from Ontario to Kansas. There are two species that look much alike and inhabit much the same territory, this one and its first cousin, the Perfoliate Bellwort. To the ordinary eye the main difference is that the Large-flowered Bellwort earns its name with flowers that are from 1 to 1½ inches in length. Since the 6 narrow yellow segments hang close together the width is not worth mentioning. The Perfoliate Bellwort has smaller flowers and smoother leaves as well as other differences of which the botanists take official note. But the Large-flowered Bellwort is just as "perfoliate" as its cousin. If you look closely, you will see that the stem of the plant grows through the bases of the leaves.

[18]

RED TRILLIUM
(*Trillium erectum*)

There is a difficulty with the Trilliums because there are so many different kinds about the country with so many overlapping names. There are a dozen or so species that may be found in the Spring woods or along shaded roadsides of almost any section of temperate North America. The plants are much alike in general appearance and growing habits, but some are larger than others, some hold their flower faces up, some let them droop, and the color differences often are striking. Any one of these many different species may be locally called a "Wake-Robin," and, indeed, there is some dispute as to just which species John Burroughs had in mind when he wrote his famous book, *Wake-Robin*. The Burroughs family tradition is that the author meant the Large White Trillium (*Trillium grandiflorum*), but the Red Trillium also is commonly called the Wake-Robin in many localities. It is sometimes called the Ill-scented Wake-Robin, for an obvious reason if you sniff the flower, and it is further known as the Purple Trillium, Wet-dog Trillium, Nosebleed, Red Benjamin, Squaw-flower, Birth-root—and Stinking Willie!

It is a fleshy plant growing from about 1 to 1½ feet in height, with 3 large somewhat heart-shaped leaves held out at wide angles from the stem at the same level and 1 flower carried on a slender stalk—or a "peduncle" if there is a botanist in the party. The 3 red or purplish petals are backed by 3 narrower bronze-tinted sepals that fill in the spaces between the petals and sometimes make it look like a "6-petaled" flower. The head of the flower tends to droop over shortly after it comes into bloom, which is about the time that the Robins come back in Spring to carol in our dooryards; hence the name of Wake-Robins for all of the Trilliums. The confusion that often exists with a number of different English names for a single flower is the reason why the botanists use Latin names for each species. It is not to show off their knowledge but to make sure of the identity of the species under discussion. The Red Trillium—if that's what you want to call it—has half a dozen other more or less accepted common names in different sections, but it has only one scientific name, *Trillium erectum*, and that is in a dead language not subject to change. The name Trillium comes from the Latin word "*tres*," meaning "three," and refers to the fact that most of the flowers of this name have three leaves, three petals, and three sepals. The added "erectum" for this species indicates that it holds its flower face skyward at blooming time—though not always! You may pass many Red Trilliums without noticing them because they are modestly hanging their heads. Be on the watch for that when you see the leaves in the Spring woods.

[19]

JACK-IN-THE-PULPIT
(*Arisaema triphyllum*)

Here we have a childhood favorite, the familiar and picturesque Jack-in-the-pulpit. It is a member of the same family as the Skunk Cabbage (the Arum Family), but it makes its appearance a little later in the season than its hardy cousin. It grows to a height of 2 or even 3 feet amid the early greenery of the moist woods all the way from Nova Scotia to Minnesota and points north, and as far south and west as South Carolina and Kansas. Its curious construction and its quaint common name combine to make it a childhood attraction. Like the Skunk Cabbage, the flowering part has a protective hood or "spathe," with a flower-bearing stalk or "spadix" within. In this case the hood forms the famous "pulpit" and the pencil-shaped, flower-bearing stalk inside the "pulpit" is the Reverend Jack at his silent preaching.

The 1 or 2 leaves, each divided into 3 large leaflets, are taller than the flowering part of the plant and often hide the Reverend Jack and his pulpit from view. The pulpit may be more or less heavily striped on the inside. Some of these plants bear only male flowers and others only female flowers, but in general the tiny and usually unnoticed flowers are clustered around the pencil-shaped "Jack" himself, the staminate flowers above the pistillate. If you keep an alert eye on the floor of damp woods in Summer, you will often find clusters of red berries on the tops of fleshy stalks. These are the remains of the Reverend Jack, the product of the fertilized pistillate flowers. The leaves wither. The pulpit droops and falls away. The clusters of red berries frequently go unrecognized in the Summer by the children who eagerly search for the Jack-in-the-pulpit of the Spring woods.

The plant is sometimes called Indian Turnip. That's because it has a turnip-shaped root that, after much boiling, was eaten by the American Indians. Do not sample it without boiling it severely or the pulp may cause a burning of the tongue and lips that will last for hours—even a day or more. The Indians also boiled and ate the red berries, which are much easier on the tongue than the root. The North American Indians were a hardy race and ate many plants and roots that the white invaders of this continent were unable to relish or digest. That's one reason why we call this plant Jack-in-the-pulpit instead of Indian Turnip. Another name for it is Starch-plant. It is a relative of the Cuckoo-pint of England from which starch was made to stiffen Elizabethan ruffs.

[20]

WOOLLY BLUE VIOLET
(*Viola sororia*)

There are blue Violets, white Violets, yellow Violets. There are Violets of the door-yard, Violets of the wet meadows, Violets of the deep woods. There are the Violas and the Pansies of the cultivated gardens, members of the same widespread family that inhabits not only most of North America but most of the temperate regions of the world. The leaves differ in many species and the flowers vary in size, shape and color, but they are all Violets and as such dearly prized wherever they are found. Poets have sung of them in many languages. They are hardy, lovely, and fragrant. Some come with the return of the birds in Spring and some linger with us on the high hills until the heat of Summer beats them down. We find them in the swamps and on mountain peaks. Some of them dare to sprout a few adventurous blooms in September or even October. It is enough for the ordinary person to distinguish the white or yellow Violet from the blue, but to go much further than that is not so much the desire of the flower lover as it is the business of the botanist who has the task of identifying all the species of a particular region. The Woolly Blue Violet is found from Quebec to Minnesota and south to North Carolina and Oklahoma.

GAY-WINGS; FLOWERING WINTERGREEN
(*Polygala paucifolia*)

This is a beautiful little pink or rose-purple flower that grows on the floor of upland woods in Spring. It is found from New Brunswick to Georgia and from Manitoba to Illinois. For a little flower it has a wide variety of names in different parts of its range. Among the names are Gay-wings, Flowering Wintergreen, Fringed Polygala, Fringed Milkwort, and Bird-on-the-wing. The roots have a delightful wintergreen fragrance that accounts for one of its many names. The plants are quite small, usually from 4 to 7 inches in height, with all the larger leaves and the 1 to 4 flowers clustered around the top of the stem. The somewhat tube-shaped flowers with a finishing fringe are about an inch long, more or less. They come into bloom in May, and in some northerly parts of their range the flowers are found as late as July. There is no other low-growing, tube-shaped, rose-purple fringed and fragrant flower in the Spring woods, so there should be no doubt about the identity of *Polygala paucifolia* if you come upon it. The only doubt will be the common name applied to it in that locality.

[21]

WILD (or FALSE) LILY-OF-THE-VALLEY
(*Maianthemum canadense*)

This abundant little Spring flower, which is a relative of the familiar Lily-of-the-valley of city florist shops and suburban gardens, grows in widespread patches on the forest floors and other shaded places all the way across the North American continent from Newfoundland to the Canadian Rockies and as far south as Georgia, Tennessee, and Iowa. It is called Wild (or False) Lily-of-the-valley because it is a small white flower growing amid much larger rich green leaves close to the ground in large patches and perhaps from a distance and at a casual glance it does bear a general resemblance to its cultivated cousin, but any close inspection will show the difference. This plant grows from 3 to 7 inches in height, and the stem, which is often zigzag, has from 1 to 3 (generally 2) lance-shaped to oval leaves that are heart-shaped at the base. Along the upper part of the stem the many little flowers jut out sidewise in what the botanists call a "terminal raceme." So if you take a good look at the arrangement of these flowers along the stem, you will have a clear idea of what a "terminal raceme" is. If you have a good eye—or a handy magnifying glass—you will see that the "face" of each tiny flower is 4-parted. They bloom in May and June, and even into July at the northern fringe of their range.

CINQUEFOIL; FIVE-FINGER
(*Potentilla simplex*)

There are so many species and varieties of Cinquefoil or Five-finger in North America that only a botanist can deal with them. The Old-field Cinquefoil pictured here is one of the more common species and may be found in fields and open woods from Nova Scotia to Ontario and Minnesota and south to North Carolina and Oklahoma. It has the 5-fingered leaves—the leaflets extended like an open hand—that are the mark of most of the clan, along with a small, 5-petaled, yellow flower. Some farm folk refer to this species as well as to the low-growing Common Five-finger (*Potentilla canadensis*) as the "Yellow Strawberry," but the Wild Strawberry has a white flower and 3-section leaves instead of the "five-finger" leaves and the yellow flowers of its close neighbors of the open fields. The Old-field Cinquefoil lifts its roving stem higher than the Common Five-finger—sometimes to a height of 18 inches—and it may reach out a yard or more with its rooting tip. You can't go far afield in Spring or Summer without finding one or other of the Cinquefoils in bloom. They are really quite pretty little flowers but they are so small that few persons notice them.

[22]

WILD COLUMBINE
(*Aquilegia canadensis*)

One of the most delicate, beautiful, and odd-shaped of our native wild flowers is the common Wild Columbine that generally grows around rocks in shaded ground and may be found in such places almost anywhere in temperate North America. The only excuse for using the word "common" in describing such a lovely flower is to distinguish it from the other native Columbines that are not so numerous nor so widespread over the country. The curious and beautiful flowers are the delightful terminal decorations of a branching plant that grows to a height of 1 to 2 feet or more. The foliage is feathery to the eye, much divided, and has somewhat mitten-shaped leaflets that are rather sharply scalloped or lobed. The odd shape of the flowers that —most of them, anyway—hang "face downward" is due to the fact that the 5 petals grow backward in tubular spurs that are highly spectacular. All the Columbines have flowers of that shape, though the different species and varieties differ in size and color as well as in haunts and habits. The species pictured here is the best known and most abundant from Nova Scotia to the Northwest Territory and south to Florida and Texas.

Rocks are not essential as a growing ground for the Wild Columbine, but it flourishes so often around or amid rocks and boulders on shady banks and wooded slopes that it is called Rock Bells in some localities. Depending upon the latitude, it flowers from April to July. The usual color combination is bright or deep red running into a cream yellow or white, but this may vary somewhat over its full range. Because of its attractiveness it is everywhere cherished and even protected by law in some areas. It belongs to the Crowfoot Family, which includes the Buttercups, Anemones, and Hepaticas with many less-known wild flowers. There is some dispute among botanists as to the meaning or derivation of the scientific name of the Columbines, *Aquilegia*. Some say it comes from the Latin word for eagle, "*aquila*," because of the fancied resemblance of the spurred petals to the claws or talons of an eagle. Others assert that it traces from "*aqua*," the Latin word for "water" and "*legere*," meaning "to collect," in reference to the little drops of sweet fluid—nectar—found at the bottom of the spurs of the Columbine petals. The lovely Long-spurred Blue Columbine (*Aquilegia caerulea*) found on shaded high ground from New Mexico to Montana is the State flower of Colorado.

[23]

WILD GERANIUM; SPOTTED CRANE'S-BILL

(*Geranium maculatum*)

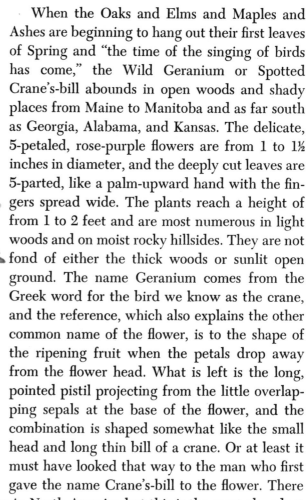

When the Oaks and Elms and Maples and Ashes are beginning to hang out their first leaves of Spring and "the time of the singing of birds has come," the Wild Geranium or Spotted Crane's-bill abounds in open woods and shady places from Maine to Manitoba and as far south as Georgia, Alabama, and Kansas. The delicate, 5-petaled, rose-purple flowers are from 1 to 1½ inches in diameter, and the deeply cut leaves are 5-parted, like a palm-upward hand with the fingers spread wide. The plants reach a height of from 1 to 2 feet and are most numerous in light woods and on moist rocky hillsides. They are not fond of either the thick woods or sunlit open ground. The name Geranium comes from the Greek word for the bird we know as the crane, and the reference, which also explains the other common name of the flower, is to the shape of the ripening fruit when the petals drop away from the flower head. What is left is the long, pointed pistil projecting from the little overlapping sepals at the base of the flower, and the combination is shaped somewhat like the small head and long thin bill of a crane. Or at least it must have looked that way to the man who first gave the name Crane's-bill to the flower. There are several other species of Wild Geranium in North America but this is the most abundant over a great part of the continent east of the Rocky Mountains.

Sometimes there is as much enjoyment in reading about flowers as there is in finding them in the woods and fields. For instance, there is in *Leaves from Gerard's Herball*, by Marcus Woodward, an account of the virtues of the Crane's-bill plant as set down by the quaint old English surgeon and gardener John Gerard, when he published his famous *Herball* in 1597. Though he was weighing the good points of a different species, doubtless he considered them family virtues and, as such, would have said or written the same things of our own Spotted Crane's-bill or Wild Geranium. Of his Crane's-bill, a cousin to our own, he wrote in part:

"The herbe and roots dried, beaten into a most fine pouder, and given halfe a spoonfull fasting, and the like quantitie to bedwards in red wine or old claret for the space of one and twenty daies together, cure miraculously ruptures and burstings, as my selfe have often proved, whereby I have gotten crownes and credit: if the ruptures be in aged persons, it shall be needfull to adde thereto the powder of red snailes (those without shels) dried in an oven. . . ."

However, such treatment is not recommended in medical books of today.

COMMON WILD MUSTARD
(*Brassica nigra*)

This is a common plant of waste places, wild fields, and road-sides all over the United States and southern Canada. It grows from 2 to 7 feet in height, is often much branched, and bears clusters ("racemes") of small yellow flowers at the ends of the branches. Like all members of the great Mustard Family, it has 4 petals. The Latin name for the family is *Cruciferae*, meaning "cross-bearing," because the 4 petals are arranged somewhat in the shape of a Maltese Cross. There may be a dozen or more flowers in each cluster but the individual flowers are only ½-inch or less in diameter. The leaves are larger at the base of the plant and grow smaller upward along the stem and branches. They are saw-toothed along the edges and usually deeply lobed or cut, many of them having the "bow-tie" or even double "bow-tie" effect along the lower part of the mid-vein. This and several other species of Wild Mustard are not native but invaders from Europe. The best-known and most useful members of the Mustard Family are such "kitchen garden" reliables as Cabbage, Broccoli, Kale, Brussels Sprouts, and Cauliflower, all of which, if they are allowed to flower, will produce clusters of yellow or whitish-yellow 4-petaled flowers much the size and general shape of those of the Common Wild Mustard shown in this picture.

PHILADELPHIA FLEABANE
(*Erigeron philadelphicus*)

The Fleabanes—and there are many of them—look like delicate downy Daisies of different pale colors and, as a matter of fact, they belong to the same great Composite Family that includes all the Asters of our fields and woods, the common White or Field Daisy, the Black-eyed Susan, and many other wild flowers. There are more than a dozen species of Fleabane that are fairly common in different parts of Canada and the United States. Though it may be locally rare or absent, the Philadelphia Fleabane is to be found from Newfoundland to British Columbia and from Florida to Texas. It grows from 1 to 3 feet high, and the "ray flowers" or silky "fringe" of the flower head may be light rose-purple, pink, or whitish. The hue is variable in the "rays," but the "disk flowers" (center circle) are always yellow. The expanded flower may be as much as an inch in diameter, but more often is something less than that. The leaves at the base of the stem may be 3 inches long and narrowish. The leaves sparsely scattered along the stem are smaller and "sessile," meaning that the base of the leaf is right on the stem. This species has a long blooming period and may be found in flower any time from April through August.

SWAMP or MARSH BUTTERCUP
(*Ranunculus septentrionalis*)

If there are two flowers that everybody knows, they are Daisies and Buttercups. There are some three dozen species of Buttercup spread over North America and the Swamp or Marsh Buttercup is just one of the many, but it is the common species found in swamps, wet meadows, and low ground over most of the United States and southern Canada from the Atlantic Coast to the Ozarks. It grows from 1 to 3 feet high, with considerable branching. Each leaf has 3 large divisions and many smaller divisions ending in rather sharp points. The spread of the 5-petaled shining yellow "cup" is about 1 inch across, and it may be found in bloom—depending upon the location—from April through July. The differences among the many native species of Buttercup concern the botanist more than they do any reader of a book like this. To the ordinary person, a Buttercup is a Buttercup wherever it is found. For centuries to come—as for centuries in the past —children will be holding the golden chalices close under the chins of their companions to tell by the yellow reflection "whether or not they like butter." The test always brings the same answer. Apparently all children like butter!

FORGET-ME-NOT
(*Myosotis scorpioides*)

The lovely little Forget-me-not has been introduced from its native Europe to the banks of ponds, brooks, and streams in the northeastern part of the United States where it may be found creeping in tangled and matted masses from which the stems reach up feebly to show their terminal clusters of tiny blue flowers with yellow centers. Tennyson wrote in his lovely poem *The Brook* (with the brook itself speaking):

> *I steal by lawns and grassy plots:*
> *I slide by hazel covers;*
> *I move the sweet Forget-me-nots*
> *That grow for happy lovers.*

The American Brooklime or Speedwell (*Veronica americana*), which grows in similar places over most of the United States, might be mistaken for the Forget-me-not at a quick glance, but it can be noted that the flower face of the Forget-me-not is 5-lobed, whereas the Speedwell's is 4-lobed. Also the leaves of the Speedwell are shorter and wider and grow in pairs on opposite sides of the stem.

CLIMBING (or BITTERSWEET) NIGHTSHADE
(*Solanum dulcamara*)

This is a vine that grows from 2 to 8 feet in length, creeping along stone walls, rail fences, or almost any kind of support. It was introduced into New England long ago from Europe and has been spreading westward and southward steadily with such success that it has been reported as far from its New England landing place as Kansas. It is a member of a remarkable family that includes the Potato, the Tomato, and other plants with fruits that are not so tasty. In fact, some are poisonous. If you ever have seen a Potato or Tomato plant in bloom, you may have noted the handsome little flower, 5-pointed, with the stamens jutting out in a bunch like a narrow cone. That's the way it is with the Climbing Nightshade, and the contrasting colors of the golden stamens and the deep violet or purple 5-pointed flower face form a striking combination that catches the eye. The leaves are what the botanist calls "hastate," meaning that near the base they have 2 little divisions, one on each side, as though somebody had made a bow tie on the "neck" of the leaf. The flowers grow in somewhat drooping sprays called "cymes" from May to September, and the fruit is a shining, red (and rather watery), poisonous berry produced in clusters. In Midsummer flowers and fruit are found in profusion together on the vines. Many birds seem to be immune to Nightshade poisoning and suffer no harm from eating the berries.

SHOWY ORCHIS
(*Orchis spectabilis*)

This beautiful and fragrant member of the Orchid Family is easily overlooked because—though it is common to abundant on many wooded hillsides from New Brunswick to Ontario and south to Georgia and Arkansas—it is a low-growing plant that may be obscured by taller neighbors.

The flowering stalk rarely reaches a height of 8 inches. The easiest way to find the flower is to look for the 2 shining leaves—about 6 to 8 inches long, slightly wider toward the outer end—that stretch upward and outward on opposite sides of the base of the stem. It is easier to spot these rich green leaves on the forest floor than it is to catch sight of the lovely purple and white flowers that, in many areas, are the first of our native Orchids to come into bloom. Depending upon where you live, look for them from late April to early June in rich woods and shaded rocky hillsides that are spillways for Spring seepage.

[27]

MOCCASIN FLOWER; PINK LADY'S-SLIPPER
(*Cypripedium acaule*)

Look for the Moccasin Flower—also known as the Moccasin Orchid, Stemless Lady's-slipper, and Pink Lady's-slipper—in sandy or rocky woods "when April melts in Maytime," though the average time of blooming might be mid-May over its full range, which extends from Newfoundland out to Manitoba and southward to Georgia and Alabama. It is a member of the Orchid Family. It sometimes surprises our citizens to know that we have many wild Orchids growing in North America, some of them rare and beautiful and some of them quite common and plain in appearance. The Moccasin Flower is among a group that is cherished for its elegance and dignity. The stalk or "scape" on which the single flower is carried grows to a height of 6 to 15 inches, and the lovely "slipper" may be 2 inches in length. There are 2 oval leaves, 6 to 8 inches in length, at the base of the flower stalk or "scape." Because lumbering operations have cut into the woods in which it used to grow and ruthless picking has lessened its numbers, the Moccasin Flower is protected in many areas either by State law, local option, or honored tradition.

YELLOW LADY'S-SLIPPER
(*Cypripedium pubescens*)

The Yellow Lady's-slipper—some persons prefer to call it the Yellow Slipper Orchid—usually is found on a lower level than the Moccasin Flower, its pink cousin of the Orchid Family. Where it moves up wooded slopes or climbs mountain ranges, it follows the water courses. The plant has a fondness for keeping its feet wet. It grows in moist woods and

thickets nearly throughout the United States—except California and Florida—and well up into Canada. It blooms a little later and grows much taller than the Moccasin Flower. It differs, too, in having a few oval leaves growing along the stem that may reach a height of 2 feet or more. Look for the Yellow Lady's-slipper in May and June but do not pick it when you find it. Leave it for others to enjoy. There are other kinds of Lady's-slippers across the country, all of them beautiful and all of them needing protection. The lovely Showy Lady's-slipper—white, with pink stripes—has been almost exterminated by ruthless picking over much of its natural range. If you know where any are to be found, don't spread the news too widely.

WILD LUPINE
(*Lupinus perennis*)

From Maine to Ontario and Minnesota and as far south as Florida the blue spikes of the Wild Lupine are held aloft in April, May, and June to a height of 1 to 2 feet in dry sandy soil. The plant likes the sun. It will move in where the ground is left bare and take over dry banks where the soil has been exposed. The Wild Lupine is a member of the Pulse or Pea Family and is related to the Alfalfas, Clovers, Vetches, the Wistaria Vine, the Locust Trees, the cultivated Sweet Pea, and the common garden product that is so often served with lamb chops and mashed potatoes. There are countless species of Lupine in North America; dozens in California alone. In this widespread species the leaf is composed of 7 to 11 leaflets 1 to 1½ inches long growing outward like spokes of a wheel from a common center. A near relative of the Wild Lupine is the beautiful little Texas Bluebonnet, the official flower of the Lone Star State. Unfortunately, it is not hardy north of Texas and, in fact, is found wild only in a comparatively small section of that vast territory. But there are other Bluebonnets and Lupines to be seen in season in almost any part of the country—all with a general resemblance—so be on the watch for them.

GOLDEN (WILD or CALIFORNIA) POPPY
(*Eschscholtzia californica*)

Only tourists or new settlers on the West Coast need to be told the name of this flower, because it is the State flower of California and its common name is California Poppy. To see it is to know it when the California hillsides are yellow with the blooms in Spring. It grows by hundreds of thousands in wide patches in uncultivated areas and is so highly prized that it has been taken into cultivation and may be found in different shades and a number of varieties in western and even eastern gardens. It grows to a height of 2 feet, and the individual flowers are carried aloft on their own little stems or "peduncles." The leaves are deeply cut and narrowly "many-fingered" like those of the Dutchman's-breeches, of which it is a not too distant relative. It's wonderful to walk along a California hillside bright with these flowers in Spring. What Wordsworth wrote of England's famous Daffodils well fits a golden horde of California Poppies in bloom:

A poet could not but be gay
In such a jocund company.

[29]

COMMON DAISY; OX-EYE DAISY; WHITE DAISY
(*Chrysanthemum leucanthemum*)

There is no need to describe the Common or White Daisy, also called the Ox-eye or Field Daisy. It is known to everybody and grows abundantly in fields and along roadsides over most of temperate North America, though it is more common in the northern and eastern sections than in southern and western areas. As common, widespread, and well-known as it is to the inhabitants of North America, it is not native to this continent. It comes from southeast Europe and Asia, but it has been here from colonial days and has become one of our most beloved wild flowers. It grows in abundance and is easily picked for a handsome bouquet. It does not fade quickly after plucking as so many wild flowers do if gathered and put in a vase. It is used to make school and college "daisy chains," and, for childhood's happy hours, it still serves its legendary purpose in telling—as little fingers pluck it apart—whether he or she "loves me" or "loves me not." It is in high favor with everyone except the farmers, who look upon it as a weed in their hayfields, occupying space and stealing sustenance from the soil that could be put to better use in providing just that many more stalks of tasty timothy hay for horses and cows. The farmers are justified in their complaint, but to the rest of us there is no more gay sight of a sunny June morning than a field of Daisies in full bloom.

Since everybody knows the Daisy, it can be used as a help in identifying lesser known wild flowers and learning more about them. For instance, the Daisy is a member of the great Composite Family, the term "composite" meaning "placed together" and referring

to the fact that what we might think to be a single flower—a single Daisy in this case—is really a grouping of many small flowers of two kinds: ray flowers and disk flowers. The disk flowers, individually too small to notice without a magnifying glass and too many to count in a hurry, form the yellow center of the Daisy. The ray flowers are the white strap-shaped or ribbon-like "rays" that grow outward in a circle around the yellow center and ordinarily are called the "petals" by all but botanists and their students. The Composite Family is the largest of all flower families and there are many differences in the family circle. The ray and disk flowers may be the same color or of contrasting colors. In some members of the family the blooms consist only of ray flowers and in others only of disk flowers.

Whether the ray or the disk flowers or both are fertile or not is another detail for the botanist. It is enough for the ordinary person to know that the common Daisy, with its delightfully attractive and easily observed arrangement of two sorts of flowers, can stand as a good representative of the Composite Family.

HAIRY SOLOMON'S-SEAL
(*Polygonatum pubescens*)

There is a smoother and larger species of Solomon's-seal than this one, but the Hairy Solomon's seal, whose lovely leaves are pale and covered with very fine hairs on the underside, is the more abundant over a wider area in North America. It is found in woods, thickets, and shaded ground from Nova Scotia to Manitoba and as far south as South Carolina. The stem grows on an arching slant from a rootstock, and the broadly lance-shaped leaves of fine texture alternate on opposite sides of the stem the length of the plant, which may reach a height of 1 to 3 feet. The tiny flower stems ("peduncles" to the botanist) grow out from the points where the leaves are joined to the stem. Such places are called "axils" and flowers that arise there are "axillary." Usually there are 2 little narrowly bell-shaped or tubular green flowers hanging beneath the stem at each leaf-joint, but there may be just 1 or even 3 or 4. The name Solomon's-seal comes from the "scars" on the rootstock left by growths of previous years. If you dig up the rootstock, you will note these marks that resemble ancient seals. King Solomon's name was borrowed—probably without permission—to add majesty to poetic fancy.

FALSE SOLOMON'S-SEAL; SOLOMON'S-PLUME
(*Smilacina racemosa*)

This is a stouter, larger, taller, more abundant, and even more widespread plant than the true Solomon's-seals to which it is a second cousin and which it does resemble in growing habit and leaf shape. But there the general resemblance ends, because the flowers of this plant are carried in a cone-shaped spray at the end of the stem (a "terminal raceme" or "panicle" to the botanist), whereas the flowers of the true Solomon's-seals are hung like wash on a line from the undersides of the stems. The False Solomon's-seal or Solomon's-plume (sometimes called Wild Spikenard) grows in wet woods, along shaded roadsides, or in moist shaded ground almost everywhere in temperate North America. The flower spray appears in May or June over most of its range but it may bloom as early as April in the South and as late as July at its northern limits. The sturdy stem, springing from a rootstock, usually grows on a slant to a height of from 1 to 3 feet, and the flower spray eventually turns into a cluster of red berries. The tiny individual white flowers are like 6-pointed stars and well worth a closer inspection than most persons ever give them.

YELLOW STAR-GRASS; GOLDSTAR-GRASS
(*Hypoxis hirsuta*)

This attractive little flower practically identifies itself. It is bright yellow or golden in color and is shaped like a 6-pointed star. It flourishes over most of the United States east of the Rocky Mountains and may be found in bloom almost any time between May and October. The plant is grasslike in appearance and grows among grasses of many kinds. Perhaps the bright little flower would be better known if it were not overtopped by so many of the tall grasses among which it modestly hides. These plants like the sun. They will grow in open woods but they prefer sunlit meadows and roadsides of dry soil. The leaves of the Yellow Star-grass look just like leaves of grass a foot or more in length, often drooping at the tips. The flowers are carried on stalks ("scapes" to the botanist) that look something like the leaves but are shorter. There may be from 1 to 6 flowers on a stalk, all springing from one terminal point, but the average number is 3 and ordinarily only one flower of each cluster is in bloom at a time. Look for them from early Summer to the beginning of Fall among the taller grasses of old fields and open roadsides, and remember that the bright flower face is only about ¾-inch in diameter and rarely reaches up more than 6 inches or so from the ground.

BLUE FLAG; WILD IRIS
(*Iris versicolor*)

There is no great need to describe this flower in detail since it is so well known in general through the cultivated members of its family that bloom in so many bewildering varieties in our gardens. There are numerous species of wild Iris in North America. They vary in color and size and other minor details, but most of them are largely blue in main color with dark streaks on the lighter touches of yellow or white in the center part of the flower segments. This species—sometimes called Larger Blue Flag—is the most abundant and the most widespread of our wild Irises and may be found in wet meadows, in marshes, along the edges of ponds and meandering streams, and in open wet places in general from Newfoundland to Manitoba and down to Virginia. The leaves are like the blade of a sword, long and narrow and slightly curved. The stem, atop which there may be one or more flowers, is circular, almost rodlike, and grows to a height of 2 or 3 feet. It comes into bloom in late Spring or early Summer.

SPIDERWORT; SPIDER-LILY
(*Tradescantia virginiana*)

This is a 3-petaled deep violet-blue flower from 1 to 2 inches in diameter carried on a plant that grows to a height of 1 to 3 feet in rich moist ground from Maine to Wisconsin and southward to Georgia and Missouri. Depending upon the location, it may be found in bloom from May to August. There are numerous buds in a group, but only one or two come to full flower at a time and the individual flowers wither quickly—often by noon of the day they open. Look for these flowers in the morning. The plant prefers shade to bright sunlight and is found most frequently in wet woods and along the shady fringes of lakes, slow streams, swamps, and ponds. The leaves are long and narrow, like small Cattails. The *Tradescantia* of its scientific name is in honor of John Tradescant, head gardener for Charles I of England, of whom it was written by Isaac D'Israeli in *Curiosities of Literature* that in 1620 he "entered himself aboard of a privateer, armed against Morocco, solely with a view of finding an opportunity of stealing apricots into Britain; and it appears that he succeeded in his design."

GOLDEN RAGWORT
(*Senecio aureus*)

This flower—also called Squaw-weed and Golden Groundsel—looks something like a small yellow Daisy and grows in ditches, swamps, and open wet places from Newfoundland and northern Quebec as far south and west as Florida and Missouri. It might be confused with some of the yellow Asters, but the Golden Ragwort blooms in May or June, which is early for any of the yellow Asters, and there are other differences, including the shape of the leaves and the size of the "disk" or central part of the flower head, which is smaller in the Ragworts. The basal leaves of the Golden Ragwort are from 1 to 6 inches long, heart-shaped and long-stalked. The upper leaves growing closely along the stem are narrower and much cut up or "indented." There may be from 5 to 15 or so flower heads in a loose cluster—called a "corymb" by the botanist—at the top of the stem, and from 8 to 18 yellow rays to each head. The flower "face" is somewhat less than 1 inch in diameter. Roughly speaking, if you see anything like a "yellow Daisy" in moist ground in May or June, it's probably the Golden Ragwort or some related species.

PINK AZALEA; PINKSTER FLOWER
(*Rhododendron nudiflora*)

One of the spectacular glories of the Spring woods is the flowering of the Pink Azalea, Pinkster Flower, Mayflower, Wild Honeysuckle, or whatever else it may be called over its range that extends from New England to Ohio and south to South Carolina and Tennessee. The branching shrub grows from 2 to 6 feet or more in height, and the flowers that come just ahead of the leaves are tubed or funnel-form (like the Honeysuckle) with a spreading outer end that flares into a 5-pointed star that may be 2 inches across. The narrow leaves, 2 to 4 inches long, are pointed at both ends. There are about a dozen species of Azalea in the United States, including the Rhododendron that has been brought into common cultivation and the lovely and now rare rose-purple Rhodora, of which Emerson wrote:

> *Rhodora! if the sages ask thee why*
> *This charm is wasted on the earth and sky,*
> *Tell them, dear, that if eyes were made for seeing,*
> *Then Beauty is its own excuse for being.*

MOUNTAIN LAUREL
(*Kalmia latifolia*)

The beautiful Mountain Laurel, much cherished throughout its range that extends from New England to Indiana and down to the Gulf of Mexico, is a shrub that varies from 2 to 20 feet in height and flourishes best in the woods and shady places, though it does venture into the open here and there. It has rather narrow, shiny leaves from 1 to 5 inches long and, blooming in May or June, bears a wealth of half-round clusters of lovely pink or pinkish-white flowers shaped like curiously dented and ribbed little bowls. Even before the flowers open they are a delight to the eye. In the bud they are a deeper pink with radiating lines that make them look like candy stars, good enough to eat. As food, however, the plant has a poor reputation; both this species and its smaller and darker-tinted relative, the Sheep Laurel or Lambkill, are known to make cattle ill. The scientific name *Kalmia* is in honor of Peter Kalm, a Swedish botanist who traveled eastern North America in colonial days and sent back botanical specimens to be classified and named by the great Linnaeus.

[34]

WILD PINK; DEPTFORD PINK
(*Dianthus armeria*)

There is an air of mild mystery about this modest but persistent little deep pink flower. It is very common, fairly widespread, and quite pretty in a small way, yet it is rather generally overlooked. Brought here by choice or by chance from Europe many years ago, it has been gaining ground steadily and has spread from Quebec, New England, and Georgia as far west as Ontario and Missouri. It's curious that it is not better known over this territory, because it grows readily in old fields and along roadsides and even pops up on lawns, where it will bloom between cuttings unless the lawn mower is kept busy. It has no great claim to fame itself, but it comes of a famous family—the Pink Family—and has some notable relatives. It is a cousin of the cultivated Carnation, of the Sweet William of the flower garden, and of the Bladder Campion and Bouncing Bet of waste places and roadsides across this country.

Another curious thing about this flower is its preferred English name of Deptford Pink. Here is a flower that is native to much of temperate Europe and it is named for a busy borough—Deptford—in England, a part of metropolitan London, a section filled with iron works, railroad shops, and shipyards on its Thames waterfront. The only claim to botanical distinction that Deptford can offer is that John Evelyn, keeper of a famous diary and author of a great work on English trees, lived at Sayes Court in Deptford from 1652 to 1694 and did considerable experimenting on trees and flowers in his gardens there.

The plant itself is grasslike in appearance. The stem, which may have 1 or 2 branches near the top, grows to a height of 6 to 18 inches with some grasslike leaves along it and a group of flower buds at the top—or at the top of each branch if it is branched. Though there may be numerous buds in a cluster, only one or two in each cluster will be in bloom at one time. The flowering season is from June through the Summer, and the rich pink 5-petaled flower is approximately ½-inch in diameter. If you look closely—better use a magnifying glass—you will see that each tiny petal is notched or "toothed" at the tip. It should be added that a small and inexpensive magnifying glass is not only a big help in trying to learn something about flowers but it also reveals strange and wonderful details of stamen and pistil construction that would be missed by the naked eye. The original cost is low, the upkeep is nothing, and it will last a lifetime. There are few things to be purchased today that will give as much pleasure and profit for the money expended as an ordinary pocket magnifying glass. When you have one, use it often. You will be pleasantly surprised at what you see—and how much you learn!

SLENDER BLUE-EYED GRASS
(*Sisyrinchium mucronatum*)

Though you might not suspect it to look at it, this is a member of the Iris Family. There are many species of Blue-eyed Grass in the United States and Canada, some of them so much alike that even the botanist has to look closely to distinguish one from the other. The one pictured here—the Slender Blue-eyed Grass—will serve as a good representative of the group. It grows in meadows, fields, and open woods from Maine to Wisconsin and south to North Carolina. The plant is grasslike in appearance—hence the name—and grows among ordinary grasses to a height of from 6 to 18 inches, but if you finger the stems or long narrow leaves, you will note a decided difference from the ordinary grasses at once. The stems and leaves of the Blue-eyed Grasses are quite stiff and flattened so as to be sharply double-edged in a small way. In this species the 6-parted violet-blue flower with a yellow center is about ½-inch in diameter and it can be found in bloom in different parts of its range in May or June. If you look at the flower under a magnifying glass, you will see that each of the 6 segments has a tiny bristle and a double notch at the tip.

DWARF WILD ROSE
(*Rosa carolina*)

There are about two dozen species of Wild Rose in North America, and most of them look much alike to the ordinary observer. The Dwarf Wild Rose, also called Low or Pasture Rose, is probably the most common of the group over the eastern half of the United States. It is found in dry rocky ground—often in upland pastures—and grows from 6 inches to a couple of feet in height, frequently much branched. The lovely flowers have a most delightful odor and one flowering bush of this species is enough to fill the vicinity with a delicate perfume. Like all of its clan, the plant is armed with sharp thorns but, for the most part, they are only at the places where the leaves branch from the stem. The beautiful 5-petaled flower is about 2 inches in diameter, and the compound leaf usually is composed of from 5 to 7 leaflets, the odd one being "terminal," meaning placed at the outer end. Note the general resemblance of the leaves and leaflets to those of the Strawberry, Blackberry, and Cinquefoil. They all belong to the Rose Family.

PITCHER PLANT
(*Sarracenia purpurea*)

This curious plant is found only in bogs, swamps, marshes, and wet soil generally. It flourishes over most of temperate North America east of the Rockies but is very choosy of its ground. You may search ten bogs of a region and find never a sign of a Pitcher Plant, and the whole floor of the eleventh bog may be covered with it. The name comes from the strange shape of the fleshy leaves that grow in a low rosette that may be 12 to 18 inches in diameter around the base of the plant. These leaves are hollowed like narrow, curving pitchers with a large pouring lip and a projecting "wing" or "flange" that might easily serve as a handle. The stiff and rather dull-colored nodding flower that rises a foot or two on a bare stalk—"scape" to the botanist—has 5 sepals and 5 petals that are purplish-brown. The Pitcher Plants are meat-eaters like the Venus Fly-trap. The insects that crawl into the hollow leaves are unable to push their way out again because of the backward-pointing stiff hairs that line the inside of the leaves. The insects eventually perish, fall into the water held by the leaves, and are absorbed as food for the Pitcher Plant. The full diet is a varied one, however. The roots find other food in the ground.

RED CLOVER
(*Trifolium pratense*)

Hail to the Red Clover! It is both useful and beautiful. It is loved by man and beast. Introduced from Europe, it now grows everywhere in North America and blooms through all the warmer months. When other flowers fail, a handsome bouquet of Red Clover can be gathered in any region free of charge. It is a sturdy member of a great family—the Pulse or Pea Family—that contributes mightily to the food supply of the world, and it may stand as a handsome and worthy representative of all the Clovers whose rooted habit it is to enrich the soil in which they grow through the slave labor of the countless millions of nitrogen-fixing bacteria they hold captive in subterranean nodules. There may be some persons who look on the Red Clover as fodder and not as a flower, but that seems snobbish at the very least. If you haven't considered it among the flowers of the field before, take a good look at the next Red Clover that you see in bloom. It is a lovely flower. In fact, each globular head of Red Clover is a collection of lovely little flowers, but it's the "ensemble" that strikes the eye and sticks in mind. Most of the Clovers are sweet and all of them are good, but the Red Clover is the "cream of the crop."

WILD CARROT;
QUEEN ANNE'S LACE
(*Daucus carota*)

Wild Carrot or Queen Anne's Lace, though not a native, flourishes all across the United States and Canada throughout the warmer months of the year and is attractive to the eye, but whether it is a beautiful flower or a detestable pest is a matter of opinion. Or of profession. An artist can look on it as a lovely flower with leaves of a delightful design, but farmers view it as a weed in their hayfields and dairymen despise it because it adds an unwanted faint flavor or aroma to the milk produced by the cows that graze on it—something like the odor of the crushed leaves of the plant, which is on the strong side. But like it or not, the Wild Carrot is with us in abundance from the first real touch of steady warm weather until the nipping frosts of Autumn lay it low. It grows to a height of from 1 to 3 feet and the flat-topped clusters of white tiny 5-petaled flowers may be from 2 to 4 inches in diameter. The leaves are feathery, much divided and subdivided to the extent that they have a fernlike appearance. If you give the flower clusters more than a passing glance, you will notice that there is often a dark spot near the center of the white circle of tiny flowers. Perhaps you have noticed such spots and thought they were insects on the flower cluster, an understandable mistake. But they are tiny dark purple flowers—one or more—and the curious thing is that they only appear, if at all, near the center of the circular cluster of their white brethren. How or why this happens is a mystery even to the botanists.

Sometimes the Wild Carrot is called Bird's-nest Plant, because, when the flowers begin to fade, the outer edge of the cluster curls upward to form a cuplike enclosure something like a bird's nest. The common or garden variety of yellow Carrot that goes into the soup or the stew is a lineal descendant of the Wild Carrot, and both are members of a famous family that includes such tasty or nutritious representatives as Caraway, Anise, Parsley, Parsnip, and Celery. The scientific name of the family is *Umbelliferae*, meaning "umbel-bearing," and refers to the family custom of producing flowers in "umbels" or "compound umbels" of which the Wild Carrot is a prime example. You will notice that the outspread supports of the flower cluster have a common starting point. Botanists call that arrangement an "umbel." If there is a further division of the same type along each one of these supports—as in the Wild Carrot—the resultant flower display is a "compound umbel."

BLADDER CAMPION
(*Silene cucubalus*)

This is a common flower of the road-sides and waste places and is a favorite with many children because of the sound effect that they get from it. Everybody knows how to blow up a paper bag and make a loud noise with it by suddenly crushing it in a way to make it "explode" under the pressure. On a small scale, children can do something like that with this flower because of the cuplike calyx behind the white petals. They pick the flower, pinch the top of the calyx closed with the thumb and forefinger of one hand, and then "explode" it by tapping it smartly against the outstretched palm of the other hand. If they have the top of the calyx pinched tightly, the resultant "pop" is considered well worth the effort. There are many other species of Campion and close relatives in North America —they are all members of the Pink Family and some are quite beautiful in color—but none equals the Bladder Campion in producing a fine "pop" under expert youthful handling.

This species is a hardy branching plant that grows to 3 feet or more in height and bears its white flowers in numerous loose clusters at the top and the ends of the branches. The flower has 5 petals but each of them is so deeply divided that it looks like 2 petals at a quick glance. Some of our Campions are natives and some have been introduced from other continents. The Bladder Campion, a native of Europe and Asia, was brought over here by early New England settlers, and, after getting well-rooted in that region, it began to spread south and west in slow but steady fashion. It may turn up almost anywhere in the United States now. It has even been reported from California. The rather narrow leaves are 3 to 4 inches long, rounded at the base, pointed toward the tip, and grow opposite one another along the stem. A handsome relative of the Bladder Campion is the Starry Campion or Widow's-frill that grows in open woods and shaded places from Massachusetts to Minnesota and south to Georgia and eastern Texas. The white flowers of the Starry Campion have their petal margins cut like a fancy fringe that is most attractive, and the leaves grow in 4's set like spokes of a wheel—"whorled" says the botanist—around the stem. There will be no doubt about this species when you find it, because the dainty fringes of the petals will catch your eye as soon as you come near them.

DEVIL'S PAINT-BRUSH; ORANGE HAWKWEED
(*Hieracium aurantiacum*)

A stranger could easily lose his way among the many yellow-flowered Hawkweeds, but the Orange Hawkweed or Devil's Paint-brush is a relief in this group because it stands out clearly with its flowers that display a mixture of yellow, red, and burnt orange. It is found in abundance from Newfoundland to Minnesota and south to Virginia, Ohio, Indiana, Illinois, and Iowa in open sunny places such as hayfields and roadsides, and it flowers from late May or early June all through the Summer or even early Autumn. The whole plant is quite "downy" or covered with tiny hairs. It has a rosette of narrowly oval-shaped leaves at the base of the flowering stem (or "scape") that rises to a height of from 1 to 2 feet or so with a cluster of flower heads at the top. The leaves in the low rosette may be from 2 to 8 inches long and are green on both sides. At a glance it can be seen that the Devil's Paint-brush belongs in the great Composite Family like the Daisy and the Dandelion, but it is more like the Dandelion in that it has no "disk flowers" like the yellow center of the Common or White Daisy but has a flower head composed entirely of individual strap-shaped flowers called "ray flowers." This is true of the Hawkweeds as a group.

There are many species of Hawkweed in North America, most of them "native here and to the manner born," but some of them, including the colorful Devil's Paint-brush, are invaders from Europe that, after a landing somewhere in the Northeast, have been pushing southward and westward slowly but relentlessly. Through June and July—at least until the clacking mowing machine comes along to cut down the hay crop—the green hayfields of New England are brightened by myriads of Devil's Paint-brushes in bloom, to the delight of the tourist or Summer boarder and the utter despair of the farmer. They take up the room and absorb the plant food that would otherwise produce good hay, which the Devil's Paint-brush is not. The hay crop is spoiled, and the farmer and his cows mourn together. In another field overrun by Devil's Paint-brushes it may be, as John Milton put it, that "the hungry sheep look up and are not fed." But who can deny the beauty of the flower?

Among the Hawkweeds with yellow flowers there are three species that botanists tell apart but ordinary country folk lump together under the common name of King Devil. To the average eye they look much like the Devil's Paint-brush except in color. The group characteristics of the Hawkweeds are not hard to recognize, but when it comes to pinning down the species the botanical battle begins. The scientific name for the group or "genus," *Hieracium*, comes from the Greek word *"hierax"* meaning "hawk," the reference being to an ancient belief that hawks ate the plant to sharpen their eyesight. When European botanists began to separate the Hawkweeds into thousands of species, subspecies, varieties, and forms, an American botanist mourned in print that "with eyesight stimulated beyond that of ancient hawks" they had brought matters to a hopelessly fine point.

[40]

RATTLESNAKE-WEED; VEIN-LEAF HAWKWEED
(*Hieracium venosum*)

This is one of the yellow-flowered Hawkweeds, but it is a native of North America and a respected inhabitant over a large area—Maine to Ontario and south to Missouri and Florida. It is quite different in appearance and habit from the yellow King Devils and the orange Devil's Paint-brush. For one thing, the Rattlesnake-weed stays modestly out of the way in dry woods. Furthermore, its famous and somewhat dreaded cousins have leaves and stalks that are covered with fine hairs that give them a fuzzy look. This is a smooth plant from its large purple-veined leaves in a rosette at the base to the dainty, yellow Dandelion-like flowers something over ½-inch in diameter that are carried on the much-branched stalk to a height of from 1 to 3 feet amid the undergrowth of dry woods from May to October. The name of Rattlesnake-weed is supposed to have originated from some fancied likeness of the purple-veined leaves to a rattlesnake's skin. It is also alleged that in old days a juice made from the leaves of this plant was used to cure the ill effects of rattlesnake bites. This lifesaving record is viewed with more than a little suspicion by the teachers in our modern medical schools.

COMMON ST. JOHN'S-WORT
(*Hypericum perforatum*)

Ancient authorities credited this plant with various marvelous properties such as the power to keep off witches or the ability to foretell marriage for maidens provided it was gathered on June 24, St. John's Day (hence its name). It was also said that the dew gathered from its flowers was good for sore eyes. We have more than two dozen native species of St. John's-wort in North America, but this introduced species from Europe is more abundant and widespread than any of the others. It grows plentifully in waste places and along roadsides and is almost a pest to the farmers in some areas. Cattle dislike it, which is one reason why it flourishes. The plant grows to 2 feet or more in height and the 5-petaled yellow flowers, roughly star-shaped and an inch or less in diameter, are clustered at the top in a loose spray (or "cyme"). If you look closely you will see that the yellow petals are much sprinkled with black dots. The little oval leaves are "sessile," or "sitting" on the stems or branches, and the plant flowers from June throughout the Summer.

ASIATIC DAYFLOWER
(*Commelina communis*)

We have native Dayflowers, but this species, introduced from Asia, is now the common one over much of New England, New York, Pennsylvania and southward and westward to Alabama and Kansas. It blooms in great abundance in late Spring and through most of the Summer in moist ground around dooryards and along the fringes of pools, ponds, brooks, and rivers. It is a low-growing plant with stems that may be 1 to 3 feet long but often grow slantwise and rarely lift themselves more than a foot or so above ground. The leaves are long and narrow, and the blue flowers appear to have only 2 petals. There is a third much smaller petal that only botanists note, but it plays a part in the story of how these flowers came by the scientific name of *Commelina*. The tale is that the great Linnaeus, who had his lighter moments when naming flowers, saw in the two fine petals and the one much less attractive petal a resemblance to a Dutch family group named Commelin. There were three Commelin brothers, of whom two were notable botanists and the other "died before he accomplished anything in botany." The common name Dayflower refers to the short life of the individual flowers that bloom only for a day and then fade away. But that's no great loss because numerous fresh flowers are coming along all Summer.

YELLOW POND-LILY; SPATTERDOCK
(*Nuphar advena*)

This is a common, widespread, and beautiful flower that should be easy to find and recognize. It is abundant in ponds and slow streams in all but the coldest parts of North America east of the Rocky Mountains and may be found in bloom from April to September

in different parts of its range. It's true that Marsh Marigolds are good-sized golden-yellow flowers that grow in swamps and along the fringes of ponds and slow streams, but where the two plants might be growing together in the same general area, the Marsh Marigold flowers will have gone to seed before the Yellow Pond-lily comes into bloom. There are other differences easily noted. The Yellow Pond-lily flower is much larger—from 2 to 3½ inches in diameter—and has a large "core" or raised center composed of pistils, stamens, and petals. What look like the petals to the ordinary observer are the 6 sepals that are, like the pistils, stamens, and petals, a glowing golden-yellow. The thick stems, large rounded leaves, and seeds of the plant are food for deer, muskrat, beaver, ducks, and other forms of wildlife.

[42]

WILD YELLOW LILY; CANADA or NODDING LILY
(*Lilium canadense*)

We walk in the ways of the gospel (according to St. Matthew) when we consider the Lilies of the field, how they grow. "They toil not, neither do they spin; yet Solomon in all his glory was not arrayed as one of these." It may be, as some botanists insist, that the Lilies of the Bible were not the flowers that we call Lilies today, but that seems a minor matter. To look on any beautiful flower is good for the soul. There are wild Lilies of many species and different colors in North America. The Wild Yellow Lily—also called Canada Lily or Nodding Lily—ranges from Nova Scotia to Indiana and southward to Alabama, and its preferred haunts are swamps, wet meadows, and well-watered fields. The stiff stem reaches a height of from 2 to 5 feet with narrow and pointed leaves, 2 to 6 inches long, growing in circles or "whorls" along it at intervals. The yellow nodding flowers—there may be any number from 1 to 16—are carried on long stalks ("peduncles" to the botanist) and hang like a "carillon" or set of bells shedding silent music on the ground below, as if to lend flowery authority to the lines of John Keats:

Heard melodies are sweet, but those
unheard
Are sweeter;

Look for the cluster of yellow, bell-shaped nodding flowers of this species in June or July, and keep an eye out for some of the other members of the family, too, for this is the time that the Lilies spread their glories abroad over a wide area in North America. Look especially for the lovely Wood Lily (*Lilium philadelphicum*) that is found from Maine and southern Quebec to Ontario and south to North Carolina and Kentucky. The Wood Lily grows in dry thickets, open woods, and clearings, reaches a height of from 8 inches to 3 feet or more, and usually holds its 1 to 5 deeply cut flowers toward the sky like cups that certainly would not hold water. The 6 segments that form the slashed cup vary somewhat in color, but usually they are a deep orange-red much spotted with purple. When these flowers grow in the open the stem is not so tall. On the moors of Nantucket they average only about a foot in height and usually carry only one flower at the top of the stem. Look also for the Turk's-cap Lily that grows taller, blooms later, and has orange-red and much spotted flowers with segments that curve sharply backward at the tips.

WHORLED LOOSESTRIFE
(*Lysimachia quadrifolia*)

This flower may be found in bloom from late June into August in open woods or along somewhat shaded roadsides from Maine to Ontario and south to Georgia and Alabama. The stem comes straight up to a height of from 1 to 3 feet and around it there are "whorls" or circles of leaves at intervals, usually 4 leaves to a "whorl," though the number may vary. Near the upper part of the stem the little yellow flowers that look like 5-pointed stars are carried outward on thin stalks from the upper sides of the leaf-joints or "axils," so that the flowers, too, are "whorled." There are many different kinds of Loosestrife in North America but none easier to identify than this species. It is abundant in many places and, though the flowers are only about ¾-inch in diameter, the whorls of leaves—and of flowers when they are in bloom—form a striking pattern. The name comes from an ancient belief that creatures that fed on these plants would "lose strife" and become peaceful, for which reason Loosestrife was fed to yokes of oxen to make the partners work in harmony. It was supposed to have a pacifying effect on humans, too, but from the record of wars down the ages and the continued madness of modern times, either the report is completely false or the human race never has eaten enough Loosestrife.

BUTTER-AND-EGGS; RAMSTEAD; TOADFLAX
(*Linaria vulgaris*)

The farmer's daughter hath soft brown hair;
(Butter and eggs and a pound of cheese)
And I met with a ballad, I can't say where,
Which wholly consisted of lines like these.
C. S. CALVERLY

Call it what you will—Butter-and-eggs, Ramstead, Toad-flax, Jacob's-ladder, Dead-men's-bones, Brideweed, Eggs-and-bacon—this bright "sunny-side-up" Summer flower, an importation from Europe, is common almost everywhere in waste places and along roadsides all up and down and across temperate North America. It grows from 1 to 3 feet high, usually in thick patches. As you can tell by looking at the "spurred" flowers, it is a close but poor relation of the aristocratic Snapdragon that blooms haughtily in so many cultivated gardens. The color scheme of the flowers that appear in spikes at the top of the stem explains the common name of Butter-and-eggs. Notice that the leaves are grasslike and the flower is tightly 2-lipped, with the "eggs" on the lower lip.

COMMON YARROW; MILFOIL
(*Achillea millefolium*)

We have some native Yarrows in North America, but the Common Yarrow or Milfoil that blooms in waste places and along roadsides across the country from June to November was brought here from Europe. It grows from 1 to 2 feet high, holding up a rather flat and seemingly white spray of innumerable small flowers that on closer inspection look like Daisies on a tiny scale. The individual flower heads with their yellow centers and 4 to 6 white rays are only about ¼-inch in diameter, but the floral spray (a "corymb" to the botanist) may be from 3 to 6 inches or more in width. The leaves, fern-like and very finely cut, give off a strong but not unpleasant odor when crushed. There are many tales of the virtues of this plant. Its scientific name *Achillea* comes from the legend that it was used to heal the wounds of the soldiers of Achilles in the Trojan War. In Merrie England of old it was believed that chewing the leaves of this plant would cure the toothache. Old wives of the Orkney Islands made tea from the leaves, and in Sweden the plant was used in the brewing of beer. And some gentlemen of bygone days dried and powdered the leaves and used them for snuff.

BOUNCING BET; SOAPWORT
(*Saponaria officinalis*)

Anyone who rambles along railroad tracks through the Summer months will find the Bouncing Bet growing in profusion along the cindery right of way. It is an importation from Europe that now flourishes mightily on railroad embankments, along roadsides, and in waste ground generally over most of the eastern and central sections of North America, and it is pushing westward steadily, infiltrating all the way out to the Pacific coast. It grows to a height of 2 feet or so on a thick stem with leaves that are rather narrow, 2 to 3 inches long, and grow opposite one another on the stem. The many 5-petaled pinkish-white flowers grow in a flattish or somewhat round cluster (another of those "corymbs") at the top of the plant, each flower being about 1 inch in diameter. The plant is a member of the Pink Family and is thus related to the Deptford Pink and the Bladder Campion as well as all the cultivated Pinks of the aristocratic gardens. The name Soapwort sometimes applied to it comes from the fact that a lather can be worked up by crushing the leaves in water, and it is said that the plant was so used for washing purposes in rural England in olden times.

MOTH MULLEIN
(*Verbascum blattaria*)

There are those who say that the Moth Mullein came by its name because moths are attracted by its flowers, but a more logical explanation in the eyes of most observers is that the flowers themselves look much like pretty moths. Take a look and decide for yourself. The plant is an importation from Europe that has made itself very much at home on this continent and may be found in old fields and waste places, on dry banks, and along roadsides all across temperate North America. It has a round stem that comes up as straight and as stiff as a lance to a height of from 2 to 6 feet, with a rosette of large oval leaves at the base and smaller leaves lessening in size and number upward along the stem

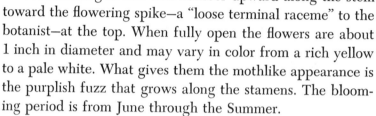

toward the flowering spike—a "loose terminal raceme" to the botanist—at the top. When fully open the flowers are about 1 inch in diameter and may vary in color from a rich yellow to a pale white. What gives them the mothlike appearance is the purplish fuzz that grows along the stamens. The blooming period is from June through the Summer.

At first glance most persons would say that the flower has 5 petals, but a botanist would not agree and anyone who has gone this far in a book about flowers may be interested in knowing why not. What look like 5 separate petals in the flower of the Moth Mullein are merely the deeply lobed or divided parts of one general corolla or petal surface around the center section of the flower. You can see this for yourself if you examine it closely. There are many flowers—like the Wild Rose or the Common Wild Mustard—that have a number of separate petals while others have the petal section united into a cup as in the Mountain Laurel or into a tube as in the Morning Glory. There are still others—including the Moth Mullein—that seem to have separate petals that turn out to be, on closer examination, the more or less deeply divided segments of what the botanist terms a "corolla." The sooner the beginner in the field learns to take note of such details the sooner he or she will be able to track down and recognize strange flowers found in walks in "fresh woods and pastures new."

Another thing that can be learned from the Moth Mullein is that the seed pods of flowers are worth looking at for several reasons. Flowers produce seed in an astonishing variety of ways and in all sorts of containers. The Moth Mullein flower produces a little round capsule that eventually splits in two and lets the tiny seeds inside fall to the ground. The Moth Mullein is a member of the Figwort Family, of which all produce seeds in much the same fashion. The empty seed pods cling to the tall stem long after flowers and leaves have gone and thus help to identify the plant.

COMMON MULLEIN
(*Verbascum thapsus*)

Here is a plant with dozens of names including High-taper, Velvet Plant, Flannel Leaf, Aaron's-rod, and, the one by which it is best known, Common Mullein. It sends up a stem that grows just as straight but even taller and thicker than that of its first cousin, the Moth Mullein, and it bears its flowers in a long cylindrical spike at the top. It grows from 2 to 7 feet in height and the leaves and stalk are covered with tiny branching hairs that give a flannel-like appearance to the large oblong leaves that often reach a length of a foot in the rosette at the base of the stem but grow smaller upward along the stem. The flower buds in the terminal spike are arranged somewhat like kernels in an ear of corn, but all the kernels in an ear of corn become ripe at about the same time whereas the individual flowers in the Common Mullein spike blossom out at intervals. What happens

is that the spike keeps growing and the upper flowers follow the lower ones in bloom. The yellow 5-segmented flowers are about 1 inch in diameter, and usually three of the stamens are "furred" with tiny yellow or whitish hairs. The resemblance to the flowers of the Moth Mullein is apparent, but the distinctive purple color of the fuzz along the Moth Mullein stamens stands out to catch the eye.

All our Mulleins are importations from the Old World. They are also all "biennials," meaning that it takes two years for them to grow to maturity and produce flower and seed. The first year the Common Mullein spreads its big jumbled rosette of large flannel leaves just above the ground, and the next season it sends up the stiff flowering stalk that country boys often use as a dueling sword or knightly lance in mimic battle. The plant likes high and dry ground and seems to be particularly fond of cow pastures. They may be found in bloom from June through the Summer months. In ancient times the dried stalks were dipped in oil or covered with tallow and used as torches in funeral processions. There was also an ancient belief that the Mulleins, properly applied, could cure diseases of the lung in man or beast and, indeed, one of the old English names for this plant is Bullock's Lungwort. But the physicians and veterinarians of today use other methods in treating any lung trouble that may afflict men, women and children or assorted farm animals.

PURPLE MILKWEED

(*Asclepias purpurascens*)

There are dozens of species of Milkweed in North America, all with the same general type of flower cluster and fruit pod and all with the family trait of oozing a sticky milky sap where there is a cut or break in flower, leaf or stem. The Purple Milkweed shown here has clusters of bright reddish-purple flowers and the midribs of the fleshy leaves are tinged with the same color. This species is found in woods, thickets, and openings from New Hampshire to Ontario and North Dakota and south to North Carolina, Mississippi, and Oklahoma. It has a rather slender stem, grows to a height of 2 or 3 feet and has somewhat tapering oval leaves that grow opposite one another in pairs or are "whorled" in 3's around the stem.

There are some Milkweeds with leaves almost as narrow as pine needles and seed pods no thicker than a fountain pen, but the Common Milkweed (*Asclepias syriaca*) found in open places from New Brunswick to Saskatchewan and south to Georgia and Kansas is noted for its stout stem, its large rubbery oval leaves, its clusters of pale purple or greenish-purple flowers, and its conical pods 3 to 5 inches long that contain the exquisitely ar-

ranged array of rich brown seeds with the silky white "milkweed down" attached to carry them off on the Autumn winds. The individual flowers are wonderful to behold. Please look at them under a magnifying glass. They are shaped like a tiny eggcup divided into 5 segments top and bottom, with 5 little caves or tunnels at the base of the top section of the cup.

The young shoots and leaves of the Common Milkweed are frequently used as pot-herbs in country kitchens, and during World War I, when the foreign fiber stuffing for life preservers on ships—kapok— was unobtainable, "milkweed down" was used as a substitute and children were paid a penny each for pods of the Common Milkweed. One of the most attractive of the Milkweeds is the Butterfly-weed or Pleurisy-root (*Asclepias tuberosa*) that grows from 1 to 2 feet high in fields and along roadsides over the eastern half of the United States and nearby Canada. The narrow, hairy leaves, 2 to 6 inches long, are not opposite but alternate along the stem, and the flower cluster at the top is a rich orange-red or orange-yellow and much favored by butterflies. Hence the name, Butterfly-weed.

FIREWEED; GREAT SPIKED WILLOW HERB
(*Epilobium angustifolium*)

Where there has been a fire in the woods or fields the Fireweed springs up to justify its name. Aside from this decided preference for burnt-over areas, it is a tall plant of waste places and roadsides all across the northern half of the United States and up to the sub-Arctic regions of Canada as well as in the cooler parts of Europe and Asia. The stout stem grows to a height of from 2 to 8 feet with many pinkish-purple or magenta 4-petaled flowers at the top in a "terminal spike" or "raceme." The lower flowers appear first, the result of which is that while the upper flowers of the spike are in bloom or coming into bloom the long narrow pods (2 to 3 inches long) left by the lower flowers that already have gone to seed are a real help in distinguishing this plant immediately from others that also display purplish flower spikes. The blooming period of the Fireweed is from July to September, and the opened flowers are about 1 inch in diameter. The plant is sometimes called the Great Spiked Willow Herb because its leaves—2 to 6 inches long—are shaped like those of the Willow Family. When the seed pods open you will notice the fine white hairs attached to the seeds and this will be a further identification mark of the plant.

WAND LOOSESTRIFE
(*Lythrum alatum*)

This is another pinkish-purple flower that appears in Summer in terminal spikes like the Fireweed, but the Wand Loosestrife is a smaller plant—only 2 to 3 feet tall—and grows in swamps or wet meadows, whereas the Fireweed is found on dry ground. Furthermore, the Fireweed flower is about 1 inch in diameter and its 4 petals are broadest at the outer ends, whereas the Wand Loosestrife flower is less than ½-inch in diameter with usually 5 or 6—though sometimes 4—narrow pointed petals. It's easy to know the Wand Loosestrife from the Fireweed, but a real problem is to distinguish the Wand Loosestrife from the Purple or Willow Loosestrife (*Lythrum salicaria*), an invader from Europe quite similar in flower and leaf. The intruder is a slightly larger and coarser plant, more or less downy, with a showier flower spike. The Wand Loosestrife is found all over the United States except in the extreme Northeast where—especially along the rivers and streams of New York and New England—the Purple Loosestrife chiefly holds sway. But the resemblance is such that, where the species overlap, it is best for the beginner to let a botanist decide which is the Purple and which the Wand Loosestrife.

BLACK COHOSH; BUGBANE; BLACK SNAKEROOT
(Cimicifuga racemosa)

This is a tall white flower of the Summer woodlands that is fairly common from Massachusetts to Georgia and as far west as Ontario, Wisconsin, and Missouri. It is easy to recognize, but confusion may start when you try to give it an English name because it lives and flourishes under so many different names in various sections of its range. Exercising local option, men, women, and children may call it Black Cohosh, Bugbane, Black Snakeroot, Rich-weed, Rattletop, Fairy Candles or anything else that comes to mind at the moment. The Latin name, of course, remains comfortably constant wherever the flower is found. The *Cimicifuga* refers to the old belief that bugs ("*cimices*" in Latin) dislike the offensive odor of the flowers so much that they hasten to fly away— in other words, become "fugitives"—when they smell it, and the *racemosa* merely means that the flowering spikes of the plants are "racemes" to the botanist. By this account the English name Bugbane would seem to have a reasonable foundation and so would the English name Black Snakeroot, because the American Indians believed that the plant would cure the ill effects of bites by poisonous snakes, but such beliefs are more legendary than factual. No doctor today would prescribe any part of the plant to cure snakebite, and certainly there are some insects that fly to it and not away from it when it is in bloom.

You can't miss this plant if it grows in your neighborhood because it reaches up above all other undergrowth in rich woods—sometimes to a height of 8 feet—and the white flower spikes are from 1 to 3 feet long and easily catch the eye "in the dim green place of the trees." The name Fairy Candles—favored in one of the present-day Wild Flower Guides— is a good indication of the general appearance of these long white spikes that are held up above the general level of the green undergrowth among which it flourishes. The tiny individual flowers look like dainty white pompons as they come into bloom not all at once but beginning at the lower part of the spike and working upward. The botanist will tell you that the tiny narrow petals are transformed stamens, but stamens and petals probably will look alike to you and they join in giving each individual flower its pompon appearance. The plant is a member of the Crowfoot Family and has the compound, saw-toothed foliage of many members of that group. It blooms from June to September, and if you miss the flowers, you may find the tall stalks later carrying the oval seed pods that, when hard and dry, make a rattling noise when the stalks are shaken. That's why the plant is known as Rattletop in some regions. Forest fires or lumbering operations may leave the Black Cohosh temporarily "without a roof over its head," so watch for it in such newly exposed areas.

BLACK-EYED SUSAN
(*Rudbeckia serotina*)

The lovely and sturdy Black-eyed Susan that grows to a height of from 1 to 3 feet along our Summer roadsides and—to the rising indignation of farmers—in our hayfields is native to North America and common from the Atlantic Coast to the Rocky Mountains. There are a number of species and varieties of *Rudbeckia*, but this is the most abundant and the best known over a wide range. It is, like the Common White Daisy, a member of the Composite Family, which means that each Black-eyed Susan is really a cluster of "ray flowers" and "disk flowers," the "ray flowers" being the circular fringe of yellow or orange-yellow strap-shaped parts that look like petals to the ordinary observer and the "disk flowers" being the tightly packed, brownish-black central part of the Black-eyed Susan. The dark central "disk flowers" are the fertile ones, and if you watch closely during the blooming period, you easily can see the tiny flowers opening and the pollen forming and ripening from the outer edge toward the center or apex of the dark cone.

The scientific name *Rudbeckia* for this attractive group of wild flowers traces back to the student days of the great Linnaeus at Upsala University in Sweden. Olaf Rudbeck the

Elder was Professor of Botany at Upsala to the time of his death in 1702 and he was succeeded by Olaf Rudbeck the Younger, who held office when Linnaeus arrived as a student, by which time Olaf the Younger was quite elderly himself. Linnaeus was poor. His clothes were shabby and he was often hungry. But he was a fine student and he wrote a paper on botany that came under the eyes of Professor Rudbeck. When the professor discovered that Linnaeus was very poor, he took the young man into his home, helped him to earn money by tutoring, and eventually launched him on a Lapland collecting expedition and a remarkable career. Those who think that Nature Study is dull or "sissified" should read the story of the stirring adventures of the young Linnaeus in Lapland. But his great work in science, however, was in devising the modern system for the classifying and naming of all living plants and animals found on earth. When Linnaeus gave the name *Rudbeckia* to the genus that includes our Black-eyed Susan, he conferred immortality on his old professor. "So shines a good deed in a naughty world" and thus is the memory of a kindly act kept green down the ages of botanical history.

HEDGE BINDWEED; GREAT BINDWEED
(*Convolvulus sepium*)

This is, as can be seen at a glance, a member of the Morning Glory (or Convolvulus) Family and many persons call it simply a Wild Morning Glory, which is not only legal but reasonably sound botanically. But the Hedge or Great Bindweed, though probably the most common and most conspicuous of the family over most of temperate North America, is only one of the dozens of species to be found in this country. The different species vary not only in the color and size of the flower but also in the size and shape of the leaves. The common flower shown here grows in fields and waste places and rambles along roadsides and hedgerows. It climbs stone walls and rail fences. The length of the blade of the leaf that is shaped like a broad arrowhead is from 3 to 5 inches, and the funnel-form flowers grow singly on long stalks ("peduncles") that come off the stem at the "axils" or leaf-joints. The main stem, which may climb straight up or run off diagonally or horizontally, may be from 3 to 10 feet long, twining around anything that will give it support. It begins to bloom in late Spring and is in flower as late as August over much of its wide range. It is a delightful decoration in waste places, but it can become something of a nuisance when it invades cultivated ground, as gardeners know.

AMERICAN WILD MINT
(*Mentha arvensis*)

Unless you search for it carefully, you probably will smell the American Wild Mint before you see it. The plant is highly and pleasantly odorous when crushed by stepping on it where it grows lushly to a height of from 6 inches to 2 feet or more along the fringes of

brooks or almost anywhere in wet soil over most of temperate North America north of the Carolinas. The small pale blue flowers appear in groups just above the places where the narrow leaves, 2 to 3 inches long, spring from opposite sides of the stem, and sometimes the flower clusters surround the stem like a ruff or with a pincushion effect. If you feel the stem with your fingers, you will notice that it is square instead of cylindrical as in most plants, and if you look closely at the tiny flowers, you will see the "two-lipped" effect of the funnel-form flower that is 5-parted at the rim, with 2 parts forming the upper lip and 3 parts the lower. These things are family traits that will help you to recognize some of the many other Mints we have in this country.

CHICORY
(*Cichorium intybus*)

This is a real roadside flower that blooms persistently but irregularly throughout the Summer along the highways and byways of this country. It is a native of Europe and the Near East that was brought here by the early colonists, who considered it a useful plant, and now it is completely at home over most of temperate North America. It grows in a somewhat staggering style to a height of about 3 feet with a stem that zigzags at awkward angles and a sparse display of raggedy leaves of no particular size or shape that clasp the stem and branches at the joints in forlorn fashion. The leaves at the base of the stem are longer and larger and somewhat on the order of Dandelion leaves, though not so numerous nor so firmly settled in place and in pattern. Cut almost any part of the plant and a milky juice will ooze out. To see these flowers is to know them because we have nothing else quite like them. Some persons call them Blue Daisies or Blue Dandelions because of the general shape and appearance of the flower heads that are, of course, a gathering of individual strap-shaped "ray flowers" as in the case of

the familiar Dandelion. The expanded flower heads, light blue to whitish in color, may be as much as 1½ inches across and the plants bloom intermittently from July to October, mostly in the open and on dry ground. The flower heads spread themselves in the morning but fade rapidly as the sun climbs the sky and are usually closed by noon.

The root of this plant, dried and ground up, is the chicory of commerce that is used as a filler or flavoring agent in coffee mixtures. There is some difference of opinion as to whether or not the addition of chicory to coffee is desirable. In the northern section of the United States most coffee drinkers like their coffee "pure and unadulterated," but majority vote in the South favors the inclusion of some chicory and most European coffee drinkers like it that way, too. The leaves of the plant are used for salad in some countries and long ago it was recorded that the Egyptians boiled and ate the root as a vegetable. In England this plant is called Succory, and in different parts of this country the blue flower heads may be called Wild Succory, Blue Sailors, Bunk, or even—to add to the confusion —Bachelor's Buttons. There seems to be no end to the confusion over the accepted English names for flowers but, to most persons, the "real" Bachelor's Buttons are the *Centaurea cyanus* of our cultivated gardens.

SEGO LILY; MARIPOSA LILY; BUTTERFLY TULIP
(*Calochortus nuttallii*)

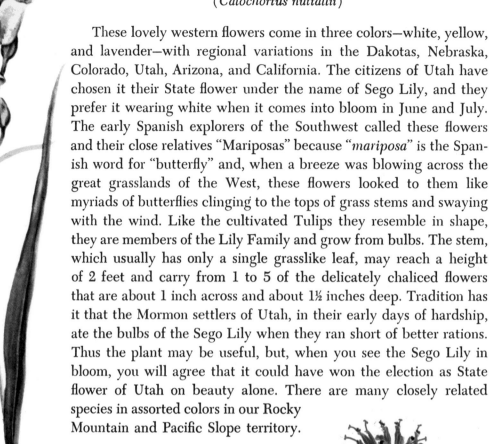

These lovely western flowers come in three colors—white, yellow, and lavender—with regional variations in the Dakotas, Nebraska, Colorado, Utah, Arizona, and California. The citizens of Utah have chosen it their State flower under the name of Sego Lily, and they prefer it wearing white when it comes into bloom in June and July. The early Spanish explorers of the Southwest called these flowers and their close relatives "Mariposas" because "*mariposa*" is the Spanish word for "butterfly" and, when a breeze was blowing across the great grasslands of the West, these flowers looked to them like myriads of butterflies clinging to the tops of grass stems and swaying with the wind. Like the cultivated Tulips they resemble in shape, they are members of the Lily Family and grow from bulbs. The stem, which usually has only a single grasslike leaf, may reach a height of 2 feet and carry from 1 to 5 of the delicately chaliced flowers that are about 1 inch across and about 1½ inches deep. Tradition has it that the Mormon settlers of Utah, in their early days of hardship, ate the bulbs of the Sego Lily when they ran short of better rations. Thus the plant may be useful, but, when you see the Sego Lily in bloom, you will agree that it could have won the election as State flower of Utah on beauty alone. There are many closely related species in assorted colors in our Rocky Mountain and Pacific Slope territory.

BEE BALM; SCARLET WILD BERGAMOT
(*Monarda didyma*)

This is the most flamboyant member of the Mint Family and such a special favorite that it is often cultivated in gardens not only because of its flaming color but also because it has the virtue of attracting Hummingbirds to probe the long floral tubes with their needle-like bills. It grows from 2 to 3 feet high in moist soil and may be found blooming from July to September over the eastern part of North America from Georgia northward. It has relatives of more conservative hues that may be found here or there all the way out to British Columbia and Southern California. The stem is "square" like that of a true Mint, and the toothed leaves, 3 to 6 inches long, grow opposite one another along the more or less hairy stem. The scarlet-hued, long-tubed flowers grow in a top ("terminal") cluster and are the crowning glory of this attractive plant. It is sometimes called Oswego Tea because the Oswego Indians are said to have made tea from its leaves.

[54]

COMMON EVENING PRIMROSE
(*Oenothera biennis*)

This is a common flower of the Summer roadsides and waste places over most of temperate North America. It prefers dry ground, including highway and railroad embankments, and is easily recognized by its stiff stem 1 to 5 or 6 feet tall, its narrow, pointed leaves growing alternately along the stem, and the terminal spike of yellow 4-petaled flowers, 1 to 2 inches across, that usually open in the evening and give their fragrance to the night air. Despite its color and its "last name," this is not the flower Wordsworth had in mind when he wrote:

> *A primrose by a river's brim*
> *A yellow primrose was to him,*
> *And it was nothing more.*

This is an Evening Primrose, quite a different family. The individual flowers appear, like theatrical stars on tour, "for one night only," but new buds open further along the spike on succeeding evenings, leaving the stiff, narrow seed capsules of previous blooms below them. There are many species showing variation in size of stem, leaf, and flower in different parts of the country and some may bloom in broad daylight.

SPOTTED TOUCH-ME-NOT;
SNAPWEED; JEWEL-WEED
(*Impatiens capensis*)

This hollow-stemmed and much branched plant grows to a height of 2 to 5 feet or more in wet woods and along the (preferably shady) sides of streams, lakes, and brooks over most of temperate North America. The numerous orange-red flowers, shaped somewhat like tiny broad-rimmed dunce caps and held at odd angles, are hung out on slender stalks (peduncles) that grow out of the "axils" or angles where the leaves appear along the stem or branches. In this species the inside of the flower is much spotted with reddish-brown. There is another much similar species, the Pale Touch-me-not (*Impatiens pallida*) with yellow flowers only sparingly spotted within. They are called Touch-me-nots in English and *Impatiens* (meaning in effect "impatient") in Latin because, when the bean-shaped seed pods ripen, the slightest touch will cause them to "explode" with a quick spiraling motion that throws the seed some distance away. Show children how to pinch the tips of the seed pods and they will have a lot of fun.

[55]

TALL MEADOW-RUE

(*Thalictrum polygamum*)

The high, white, and feathery flower clusters of the Tall Meadow-rue practically command attention when they are in bloom from June through August in moist or wet ground over most of the eastern half of temperate North America. The plant rears itself to a height of from 3 to 11 feet—averaging 5 to 6 feet—and is common in wet meadows, along the borders of swamps, and in moist ditches along roadsides over its range. It often follows the winding ways of brooks through low meadows. It flourishes in sun or shade but prefers rather open locations, where, in Summer bloom, it stands "divinely tall, and most divinely fair." You can't miss it in season, whether you are afoot, in an auto, or speeding across the countryside by train.

The leaves, light green above and paler below, are much divided and subdivided into gracefully scalloped or lovely lobed leaflets that are as tender in texture as they are attractive in appearance. The peculiar thing about the cream-white or pure white flower clusters —they may be "racemes" or "panicles" to the botanist, depending upon the arrangement of the particular clusters—is that the color is not provided by petals but by the white filaments or "shafts" of the stamens of the little individual flowers, which have no petals at all. By this time the reader will have realized that petals are not essential to all flowers either for beauty or utility, that other parts of a flower may be as attractive as petals, and that what look like petals to the ordinary eye may be something quite different to the botanist.

A close relative of the Tall Meadow-rue is the Early Meadow-rue (*Thalictrum dioicum*) that grows to a height of from 1 to 2½ feet in rich woods and damp ravines from

Quebec to Ontario and Minnesota and south to Georgia and Alabama. It is often a neighbor to the Red Trillium and comes into bloom at about the same time —April and May—but its sprays of greenish or greenish-yellow flowers, with drooping stamen filaments, do not catch the eye as easily as the white sprays of its taller cousin that blooms much later in the season and out in the open. But the foliage of the two species is of the same general design—compounded in series of 3's with leaflets that have scalloped outlines or graceful lobes—and the final proof of relationship will be the individual flowers that, with their drooping green or greenish-yellow filaments, look like little silk tassels. The Meadow-rues are a widespread group and our many species in North America have close relatives in such far places as the hill country of India and the plains of South Africa.

[56]

PICKERELWEED
(*Pontederia cordata*)

This is a blue flower that often appears in wide patches in swamps, bogs, and slow water courses all the way from Nova Scotia to Ontario and Minnesota and south to Florida and Oklahoma. It grows in abundance in shallow ponds and along the banks "of weedy lake, or marge of river wide," and blooms through the Summer months until the cold nights of approaching Autumn cut it down. It usually shows just a single large, shiny heart-shaped leaf above water and, reaching well above it, the stout stem may carry the spike of blue flowers to a height of 4 feet, though about half that would be nearer the average. The individual tubular flowers, which are numerous on the spike, are 2-lipped at the outer end and each lip is divided into 3 narrow segments. You may need boots or a boat to inspect the flower closely. The common name of Pickerelweed refers to the fact that the plant and pickerel frequently are found in the same shallow waters. The *Pontederia* of its scientific name is a tribute to an Italian botanist, Giulio Pontedera (1688–1757), who taught at the University of Padua, and the *cordata,* meaning "heart-shaped," refers to the leaf. It is said that only muskrats find the plant edible, but the spikes of blue flowers are a joy to everyone who sees them.

FRAGRANT WHITE WATER-LILY
(*Nymphaea odorata*)

There are two common—and very beautiful—species of white Water-lily found in lakes, ponds, and still or slow-moving waters over much of the United States and nearby Canada but the Fragrant or Sweet-scented is the more abundant and the more widespread of the two. The other is the Tuberous White Water-lily (*Nymphaea tuberosa*) and, where they occur in the same waters, it is sometimes difficult to know them apart. The Fragrant White Water-lily has a delightful odor, whereas its rival has hardly any perceptible scent, and the

fragrant species may be either white or pink or white with a pinkish tinge, whereas the Tuberous White Water-lily is always pure white. But it really doesn't matter (except to the botanist) which is which; the flowers are lovely decorations on our inland waters and their large circular leaves give aid and comfort to the frogs that sit on them to survey the watery world around them with a placid air of complete and well-fed contentment.

[57]

FRINGED LOOSESTRIFE
(*Lysimachia ciliata*)

This is another and one of the most widespread of the many Loosestrifes found abundantly in North America, but it grows in places that are somewhat off the beaten paths and thus avoids public notice to some extent. The Fringed Loosestrife likes moist ground and a little shade. It grows by preference in damp thickets and the drier parts of swamps to a height of from 1 to 4 feet or more, and it ranges over almost the entire United States and southern Canada. Depending upon latitude and altitude, it may be found in bloom from early June through August and its handsome 5-parted yellow flowers may be as much as 1 inch across. Notice that the ovate leaves (2 to 6 inches long) grow in pairs opposite one another along the stem and that the flower stalks ("peduncles") spring from the "axils" or leaf-joints at these points. Under a magnifying glass you can see that the leaf stalk or "petiole" is fringed with fine hairs that account for the English name of "Fringed" Loosestrife for the plant and also for the *ciliata* in its scientific name, "cilia" being fine hairs such as eyelashes or the

threadlike appendages that fringe many microscopic creatures and furnish motive power for them in water. Another detail to observe is that each of the yellow segments of the flower is finely toothed at the outer edge and there is a tiny tip that sticks out like a bristle. There may be up to half a dozen buds in a flower cluster, but usually only one or two of the cluster are in bloom at a time.

The shape and size of the leaf, the "fringed" or hairy petioles, the size of the flower, and the bristle tip to each petal segment will help to distinguish the Fringed Loosestrife from any of its close relatives that may be blooming in the same area. One of its relatives with which there is no danger of confusion is the low-growing Moneywort (*Lysimachia nummularia*) that hugs the ground on a creeping stem 1 to 2 feet in length and has roundish leaves about 1 inch in length growing opposite one another in pairs at short intervals along the stem. The yellow flowers are about the size of those of the Fringed Loosestrife, but the petal segments lack the outer teeth and bristle tip. The Moneywort is an invader from Europe that is now found from Newfoundland to Ontario and south to Georgia and Kansas. In swamps you will find the Swamp-candles (*Lysimachia terrestris*) with their conical terminal sprays of little star-shaped yellow flowers.

YUCCA; SPANISH BAYONET; OUR-LORD'S-CANDLE
(*Yucca filamentosa*)

This is probably the most familiar of the Yucca group that runs to about a dozen striking species in Central America and the warmer sections of North America. In general they are all called Spanish Bayonets (or Spanish Daggers) because of the long, narrow, sharp-pointed leaves that do look much like bayonets or sword blades and often are formidable objects with which to collide or even touch. The narrow leaves and the tall flowering spikes that raise themselves aloft are common to all the group. The leaf arrangement and the flower colors vary in the different species, and the time of blooming depends on the species and the area in which the plants are found. This species is often found in cultivation or as an escape from cultivation over much of the United States, but in the wild it flourishes in sandy soil, dunes, old fields, and pinelands from the Gulf Coast northward to southern New Jersey. Wherever it grows it is sure to catch the eye with its alarming rosette of leaves around the base and the sturdy flower-bearing spike ("peduncle") that may reach a height of 10 feet or more bearing a great "plume" of cream-white, 6-parted, pendulous, bell-shaped flowers innumerable in quantity.

Aside from the bayonet-shaped leaves and the spectacular sprays of flowers, there is another notable feature of the Yucca group. The flowers of the Yuccas are in their most expansive mood from dusk to dawn and, being mostly white in color, they are easily found by night-flying insects. There is a curious bond between the Yuccas and a small group of night-flying insects, moths of the genus *Pronuba*. Just as Bumblebees are needed to fertilize Red Clover blossoms, Pronuba Moths are needed to fertilize the Yucca flowers and no substitutes in the insect world are acceptable. Not only that, but it has been discovered that different species of Yuccas may have their own particular species of Pronuba Moth to carry the pollen from stamen to pistil. It's the female moth that does the good work and it also lays its eggs in the flowers. The larvae—the moths in the caterpillar stage —feed on the Yucca seeds, but enough seeds escape eating to carry on the species. It's an odd cycle—the flowers providing food and lodging for the moths and the moths being the necessary agents in the continued production of Yucca flowers.

CORN COCKLE
(Agrostemma githago)

Farmers and gardeners often have very definite ideas of the difference between "flowers" and "weeds," but botanists pay little heed to such fine distinctions. An old definition had it that "a weed is a flower out of place." A more modern definition, in a fair-sized dictionary, runs as follows:

"WEED, noun. 1. Any unsightly or troublesome plant that is at the same time useless; especially, a plant that is noxious or injurious to crops."

But who is to say which plants are "sightly" and which ones are "unsightly"? And what does the term "useless" imply in the definition? Useless to whom? A plant that is of no direct use to a farmer may be very useful to birds or insects that, in turn, may be useful in the production or the protection of farm crops. The Corn Cockle is often called a weed and certainly looked upon as a weed by farmers when they come upon it in their growing grain fields or "hand in hand with Plenty in the maize," to borrow a poetical sheaf from Tennyson. But who can deny the beauty of this pink or rose-purple flower? It is another of the European invaders that have found this country to their liking, and it has spread rapidly in all directions. It is found not only as a trespasser in grain fields and where the tall corn grows, but as a wanderer along the roads and a camper in waste places over most of temperate North America. It belongs to the Pink Family, along with the Bladder Campion, the Bouncing Bet or Soapwort, the Deptford Pink, and many others of our common wild flowers.

This plant grows from 1 to 3 feet in height with narrow grasslike leaves paired off on opposite sides of the stem like other members of its family. Almost all parts of the plant except the petals are covered with fine hairs. The 5-petaled flowers are 1 to 3 inches across when fully open, and they are carried on stiff stalks (or "peduncles") that emerge from the stem at the leaf-joints, which means that they are "axillary." An easily noted feature of this flower is that the sharp-pointed calyx lobes—5 in number—jut out far beyond the petal circle. The plant may be found in bloom from June into September. As for the question of whether or not it is an unwelcome "weed," let each farmer or property owner decide that for himself. Here it can be looked upon as a beautiful flower of our fields and roadsides.

[60]

STEEPLEBUSH; HARDHACK
(*Spiraea tomentosa*)

Those who know the Spiraeas of the cultivated flower gardens will have no trouble recognizing their many relatives in the wild. There are more than a dozen species native in North America, and, of the group, the Steeplebush or Hardhack is probably the most widespread east of the Rockies and the easiest to recognize because of its abundance, its sturdy stem, its upright character, and its rich wine-purple color. It grows to a height of 1 to 4 feet from July to September in old fields and unused pastures. It likes the open sky above it but otherwise is not particular and will flourish from low wet ground up across high, dry, and rocky territory. The toothed leaves, 1 to 2 inches long, circle the stem closely up to the terminal cluster of many tiny flowers. The Meadowsweet or Quaker Lady (*Spiraea latifolia*) is found over much of the same area but its leaves are a little broader, its flowering cluster is not so pointed or steeple-shaped, and its color is usually white or pinkish. If there is any doubt in your mind, look at the underside of the leaf. The Meadowsweet leaf is smooth beneath, whereas the underside of the Steeplebush leaf is covered with what looks like brownish-pink wool.

WILD SUNFLOWER
(*Helianthus giganteus*)

Leave to the botanist the task of sorting out the many different species of native Sunflowers that burst into bloom all across the country in late Summer or early Autumn. This particular species flourishes from Quebec to Florida and roams westward as far as Saskatchewan and Colorado. It grows in swamps, wet meadows, and moist ground generally and may be any height between 3 and 12 feet. The flower head, which is a collection of central "disk flowers" and a fringe of bright yellow "ray flowers," may be 2½ to 3 inches across. The leaves are 2 to 6 inches long, narrow and toothed along the edge. The name Sunflower comes from two Greek words, "*helios*," "the sun," and "*anthus*," "flower." The garden or dooryard Sunflower that furnishes most of the seed so much appreciated by certain birds is the *Helianthus annuus* of the botanist or nurseryman. It originally came from Peru and is now cultivated all over the world. Sunflowers do like sunlight and naturally the flower heads turn toward the source of light but Thomas Moore let his poetic fancy roam a bit in the lines:

As the Sunflower turns on her god, when he sets,
The same look which she turned when he rose.

[61]

BROAD-LEAVED ARROWHEAD
(*Sagittaria latifolia*)

There are more than three dozen species of Arrowhead or *Sagittaria* to be found growing in shallow waters across North America, but this is the most abundant, the most widespread, and, to most eyes, the prettiest of the lot. Where you find the Pickerelweed, there you will find the Broad-leaved Arrowhead, a plant well deserving the name it bears because the shape of the leaves that show above water—very decidedly in this species though not at all in some others—is that of an exaggerated arrow head. This same plant, however, has underwater leaves that are long and narrow like blades of grass. The leafless stem or "scape" on which the flowers are carried may project above water from a few inches to 4 feet or more and the flowers appear in little circles or "whorls" of 3's at intervals along the scape. The conspicuous male flowers, probably the only ones you will notice, have 3 white petals and are about 1 inch across when fully spread. The female flowers are smaller and

duller and usually grow below the male flowers on the scape, though there may be plants that produce only flowers of one kind, male or female. For the most part, the female flowers usually go unnoticed except by botanists or the insects that carry the pollen from the stamens of the male flowers to the pistils of the female flowers, a most important function. The dainty white male flowers—and the dull female flowers, too—begin to appear in July and may be found in bloom through August and September.

This plant is sometimes called Swamp Potato or Duck Potato because of the potato-like tubers produced along its submerged root system. Ducks, geese, and swan feed with gusto on these tubers, though sometimes they are buried so deep in the mud that only the larger and stronger waterfowl can dig them up. But the lovely Wood Duck, the most colorful bird in North America, feeds on them, and, among the diving ducks, the Canvasback rates them just behind Wild Celery as a delicate article of diet. Indeed, the American Indians boiled and ate the tubers, and history has it that the early colonists, when they were hard pressed for food, took a tip from the Indians and did likewise. But it must be admitted that the colonists abandoned such food when their own crops yielded them tastier table dishes.

GREAT BLUE LOBELIA
(*Lobelia siphilitica*)

The distaste most persons have for getting their feet wet—at least when they are wearing shoes—is probably the reason why the Great Blue Lobelia is not a more familiar flower to all of us. This sturdy member of the Lobelia group is found over most of the United States east of the Rocky Mountains, but it grows most frequently in moist soil or wet places, often along brooks and streams or around the edges of ponds and lakes. Furthermore, though it sends up a stiff stem to a height of from 1 to 3 feet or more, it is inclined to hide away among other plants of approximately similar height and, in lush growths in shaded or half-shaded places, it may be easily overlooked despite the terminal spikes of inch-long tubular blue flowers. Not only is the flowering spike often semi-obscured by surrounding greenery but each flower of the spike is buttressed by a green leaflike "bract" that helps to conceal it. Another point is that blue as a color does not stand out like red, orange, yellow, or white against a green background. All of which helps to explain why so many Great Blue Lobelias are born to blush unseen in rural regions where they have long flourished and where they flower regularly each August or September.

The Lobelias are world-wide in distribution, and there are more than two dozen species in North America. They were named after a Flemish botanist, Matthias de L'Obel (1538–1616). Among the common features of the group are a milky juice that is very bitter and indeed poisonous, leaves that grow alternately—that is, not opposite one another—along the stem, and tubular flowers that are, for the most part, 2-lipped with the upper lip split into 2 segments and the lower lip into 3. The flowers of the Mint Family are 2-lipped also, but the lip segments of the Mints are gently rounded like lobes whereas those of the Lobelias are sharp like teeth. Other differences are that the Mint leaves grow opposite one another along their stems and practically all Mints are strongly aromatic when crushed, which Lobelias are not.

A first cousin to the Great Blue Lobelia is the Indian Tobacco (*Lobelia inflata*) commonly found along the roadsides of North America from Nova Scotia to Saskatchewan and south to Georgia and Arkansas and just as commonly overlooked because its pale blue flowers, shaped like those of its distinguished relative, are small and inconspicuous. In fact, the inflated seed pods later are more often noticed than the flowers. The Indians are said to have smoked the dried leaves, hence the name.

CARDINAL FLOWER; RED LOBELIA
(*Lobelia cardinalis*)

This spectacular flower—the most brilliant in hue of the many Lobelias that flourish in North America—is easy to recognize when you see it, but the difficulty is to find it and come upon it close at hand. Like most of the Lobelia group, it prefers to keep its feet wet and usually is found growing along water courses or in fairly moist ground. Often it is sighted just out of reach along the fringes of rivers, lakes, and streams. If you have luck, you may find it growing in flaming patches in the gravelly shallows of some farm brook meandering around and about the open meadows. In such places you can get close to the flowers dry-shod and notice that, though the color is in striking contrast to that of the Great Blue Lobelia, the general shape of the two flowers is much the same. As a matter of fact, the two plants are much alike in stem, leaf, and general habits of growth. The Cardinal Flower ordinarily is the taller, growing from 2 to 5 feet high, and the individual flowers are not only usually larger but much more deeply "slashed" than those of the Great Blue Lobelia. Another difference is the Great Blue Lobelia is more modest than its brilliant cousin. For the most part, it keeps in the shade if possible. But the flaunting Cardinal Flower is not one to hide its beauties. It lifts its flaming clusters of 2-lipped scarlet flowers in sunny places and seems to clamor for attention. The added touch of sun may be one reason why it comes into bloom in July, whereas the Great Blue Lobelia usually waits until August to spread its first floral display of the season. Both species bloom through August and into September.

Scientists tell us that birds prefer red as a color and insects—especially bees—prefer blue. There is more in that than meets the eye, but, not to go into it too deeply, the Great Blue Lobelia is constructed so that it is fertilized by the bees that push their way into it for food and eventually carry the pollen from stamen to pistil as they journey from one blossom to the other. But the pistil and stamens of the Cardinal Flower are so placed that it's no trouble at all for Hummingbirds to perform that same useful purpose. Hummingbirds are particularly attracted to red flowers and, with their long thin bills, are admirably fitted for sipping nectar from tubular blossoms like those of the Cardinal Flower. Furthermore, they love to forage up and down sunny brooks, where these flowers often grow. If there are Cardinal Flowers in bloom, the Hummingbirds will find them. It's a mutual benefit association. These brilliant flowers range widely in North America and may be found from Quebec to Ontario and Minnesota and south to Florida and east Texas.

[64]

PEARLY EVERLASTING
(*Anaphalis margaritacea*)

This is one of the most dainty and satisfactory of the wild flowers because it is easy to find, easy to know, and easy to gather in a bouquet that will keep if not everlastingly, at least for many a long day. It grows in upland pastures and on dry open hillsides all across the northern half of North America almost up to the Arctic snow line. The stem, topped by the spray of pale flowers that look so delicate and persist so sturdily, grows from 1 to 3 feet in height with longish, narrow, grasslike leaves of somewhat silky texture appearing at intervals along it. It blooms through the late Summer, and Thoreau referred to it as "the artificial flower of the September pastures." The flowering arrangement is doubly compound. The whole spray is made up of numerous flower heads, and the flower heads, in turn, are groups of tiny individual flowers. The Pearly Everlasting is a member of the Composite Family, the great group that includes the Goldenrods, the Daisies, the Joe-Pye Weed, the Ironweed, the Sunflowers, the Asters, and many other common flowers.

PURPLE MILKWORT; PURPLE CANDYROOT
(*Polygala sanguinea*)

This is a modest little flower that is easily overlooked, even though it blooms all through the Summer in fields and meadows and along roadsides from Nova Scotia to Ontario and Minnesota and as far south as the broad belt extending from South Carolina to Louisiana and Oklahoma. It grows only to a height of from 6 to 15 inches on a slender stem that often forks near the top so that 2 or more flower heads are carried on one main stem. The flower heads, of course, are clusters of many tiny individual flowers, as you will note if you bend over and look closely. The short grasslike leaves, the pale purple (sometimes greenish) flower spike, and its lowly estate combine to keep the Purple Milkwort or Purple Candyroot from general recognition and a hearty welcome each year. It has somewhat the appearance of a thimble-shaped, pale purple Clover head, but the grasslike leaves prove immediately that it is not a member of the Clover group. It has a delicate bearing, but it stands sturdily through the heat of Summer and blooms well into September in favorable locations. It forces itself on nobody's attention, but it is a lovely, soft-hued, friendly little flower that is well worth your acquaintance. It is called Purple Candyroot by many persons because of the wintergreen flavor of the crushed root.

[65]

PASTURE THISTLE
(*Cirsium pumilum*)

As the Rose is traditionally the national flower of England, so the Thistle is the badge of Scotland. But Thistles of several hundred species are found scattered all over the Northern Hemisphere, and there are some 60-odd species native to North America. They are notable, of course, for the sharp prickles that stick out from the leaves and other parts of the growing plant and also for the "thistledown" that appears at the end of the blooming season of the truly beautiful flower heads. Here we have another member of the great Composite Family in which many individual flowers are clustered closely to give a striking mass effect. Most Thistles have purple flowers, but there are some species that come in pink, yellow, cream, and white. Thistles are hardy plants, and their prickles protect them from grazing cattle that cut down unarmed flowers in pasture lands. It is useless for a beginner to try to sort out the Thistles in any area. That's a task for the botanist, or at least a student in botany. But even a beginner will notice that there are different kinds of Thistles here and there.

INDIAN PIPE
(*Monotropa uniflora*)

The walker in the woods may come upon a little colony of Indian Pipe almost anywhere in North America. It is a "saprophytic" plant, meaning that it feeds on decayed organic matter, and, lacking the green coloring matter (chlorophyll) of most other plants, it has a fragile, pale, ghostlike appearance. There is a real flower at the top of the stalk or "scape," but usually it hangs like a bowed head and you will have to turn it up to see that

it is narrowly cup-shaped and there may be 4 or 5 petals, or even 6. The only touch of color about the plant is the yellow of the pollen in its brief period of ripening. Except for that, flower and scape and buried roots are a fleshy, sickly grayish-white. It rarely reaches a foot in height and the stem looks something like a pale, emaciated asparagus stalk. You may find these odd flowers pushing up from the forest floor in little groups almost any time from June through September. False Beech-drops, a near relative, grow a little taller, are tawny or brownish-yellow, much thicker in stalk, and sometimes venture so far out of the woods that they may be found in shady spots on lawns.

[66]

TURTLE-HEAD; SNAKE-HEAD
(*Chelone glabra*)

Here we have another common flower that is well-named. The individual blossoms, viewed from the side, do look something like the head of a turtle or a snake with its mouth open for business purposes. There is a pink species (*Chelone obliqua*) southward, but the common one over most of eastern North America is the cream-white Turtle-head that is pictured here. It's a sturdy plant that flourishes along the fringes of streams, swamps, wet meadows, and roadside ditches and grows to a height of 2 to 5 or even 6 feet on a stiff stem with the flowers closely bunched in a blunt spike at the top. The flower buds may be numerous, but they do not all open at the same time. In keeping with the usual procedure when flowers are carried in such spikes, the lower flowers open first and the order of blooming is upward. The long narrow leaves, shaped like a lance head, grow opposite one another, are toothed all around, and are so short-stalked (or "petioled") that they seem to be growing right out of the stem. The time to look for Turtle-head in bloom is from late July until the first hard frost.

Turtle-head is a member of the Figwort Family and, as such, a relative of the common Butter-and-eggs or Wild Snapdragon. You may notice something of a family resemblance in the shape of the flowers. Another member of the same family is the Smooth White Penstemon or Foxglove Beard-tongue (*Penstemon digitalis*) with a pale lavender or nearly white flower that might possibly be confused with the Turtle-head by beginners. This is only one of the dozens of Penstemons in North America, but it seems to be gaining ground in all directions. A native of the Mississippi Basin, it has spread to South Dakota and Texas on the west, has reached Virginia on the east, and has been pushing boldly into New England in recent years. It grows to a height of 5 feet or so in groups and patches in open woods, thickets, and fields, but its tubular flowers, though somewhat like those of the Turtle-head in size and general shape, are more open at the outer edge and definitely 5-parted. But the big difference is that, where the Turtle-head flowers sit close along a blunt terminal spike, the Smooth White Penstemon flowers are carried well apart in a loose spray (a "thyrsus" to the botanist) with each flower on a stalk or "pedicel" 1 to 3 inches long. Also, the Turtle-head flower is a solid cream-white, whereas the Smooth White Penstemon flowers look as though they might be made of waxed paper or frosted glass.

[67]

WOODLAND GERARDIA
(*Gerardia tenuifolia*)

These lovely rose-purple flowers of late Summer and early Autumn—light in color and delicate in texture—are displayed like ornaments on a Christmas tree in scattered sprays or "racemes" on a widely branched plant of many thin branchlets and short thin leaves that look for all the world like misplaced blades of grass. The plant grows only to a height of a foot or so and is shaped somewhat like a miniature apple tree; that is, with a short trunk or "bole" and a widely spread "head," all on a scale so delicate that, with its thin branchlets, its narrow and sparse leaves, and its featherweight rose-purple flowers, it might almost be an "airy nothing" to which some poet gave "a local habitation and a name." Indeed, the Gerardias one and all are named for wonderful old John Gerard, the great English botanist who published his famous *Herball or General Historie of Plants* back in 1597 and included in it such helpful botanical and medicinal hints as that the juice of an Onion rubbed on a bald head in the sun "bringeth the haire againe very speedily" and the juice of the Daisy "given to little dogs with milke, keepeth them from growing great."

There are many species of Gerardia in North America, all of them having a family resemblance in flower shape and general delicate texture of the plants, but they vary much in size and color. The Woodland Gerardia is found from Maine to Michigan and, inland from the Atlantic coastal plain, south to Georgia and Louisiana. It grows in dry woods, thickets, and fields and blooms from August to October. Although the individual flowers —something less than an inch long—are narrowly bell-shaped, they do not hang as bells should but usually are held throat upward or horizontal. The outer rim of the corolla is 5-lobed with more than a hint of a 2-lipped formation. The delicate flowers fade by noon of the day they open, but new buds provide a fresh supply for succeeding days and the plants may be in bloom for the better part of three months. A similar member of the Gerardia group but slightly larger in every way is the Purple Gerardia (*Gerardia purpurea*) whose flowers may be 1½ inches long. The plant itself grows to a height of 3 feet or more and is more an inhabitant of moist soil and wet meadows than the Woodland Gerardia. It is found from New England to Minnesota and south to Florida and Texas and blooms from late July through September.

EARLY GOLDENROD; PLUME GOLDENROD
(*Solidago juncea*)

Leave to the botanists the tedious task of sorting out the hundred or more species of Goldenrod that are native to North America. The flowering sprays of this abundant group are known to everybody and feared by many persons as the cause of "hay fever," but the truth is that Goldenrod is no more guilty than any other plentiful plant that produces pollen. Medical research has revealed that, over most of the United States, the Great Ragweed (*Ambrosia trifida*) is the real guilty party in most cases, and it doesn't have the compensating virtue of the glorious beauty of the Goldenrod in late Summer and Autumn. Asters and Goldenrod make lovely the meadows and hillsides "when the frost is on the punkin and the fodder's in the shock."

The group name *Solidago* is derived from the same Latin word that gives us "solidify," to make whole, and refers to the healing powers that ancient physicians believed the plants to possess. John Gerard wrote in his famous *Herball* of the Goldenrod: "It is extolled above all other herbes for the stopping of bloud in bleeding wounds."

Goldenrod is well-named, because most of the stems are rodlike and serve nobly to hold up the attractive sprays of countless tiny golden flowers—with one notable exception in the case of the Silver-rod (*Solidago bicolor*) whose white or whitish flowers make it the pale member of this glowing group. You will find it growing among its golden brethren in dry ground over most of the United States east of the Rockies, and probably you will think it "a poor stick" in comparison with its richer relatives because its straight stem carries no flaunting flower spray. Its whitish flower heads merely cling somewhat forlornly along the upper portion of "rod." The Early or Plume Goldenrod shown here is found from New Brunswick to Saskatchewan and southward to Georgia and Missouri. It grows to a height of 3 feet or more in dry open ground, and its fine plume of golden flower heads may be found in bloom from late June to October. Remember that the Goldenrods are members of the great Composite Family and that the golden sprays are masses of flower heads that are, in turn, made up of tiny "ray flowers" and "disk flowers" best seen under a magnifying glass. But it's the general effect that is so colorful in our Autumn landscapes.

BONESET; THOROUGHWORT
(*Eupatorium perfoliatum*)

This sturdy plant with the medicinal name grows to a height of from 2 to 5 feet over most of temperate North America east of the Rocky Mountains and spreads its flat-topped clusters ("corymbs" to the botanist) of whitish flower heads for inspection from late July well into October. It grows in wet places generally—in swamps, along the fringes of streams, in ditches, on well-watered banks, and along woods roads where the overhanging trees keep the roadsides shady and moist. The grayish-white flower spray at the top of the plant may be as much as 6 inches or so in diameter and has something the appearance of a flat-topped white Goldenrod. But to the ordinary eye the most curious thing about the plant is the way the stem seems to grow right through the leaves, particularly the lower and larger ones that are completely joined at the base and reach out on opposite sides of the stem like a pair of narrow-based triangles from 4 to 8 inches long. The English name Thoroughwort often applied to this plant is a reference to this habit of the stem growing "thorough" or through the leaves, and so is the *perfoliatum*—Latin for "through the leaf"—of its scientific name. There are various explanations of how the plant came by the common name of Boneset. Some authorities have it that "herb doctors" declared that plants with united leaves like this one had the virtue of aiding to unite fractured bones. Another story is that an infusion made from the leaves of the plant was reputed to be good for the dengue or "break-bone" fever of warm climates; hence the name Boneset. In any event, "Boneset tea" made from the dried leaves was a standard home remedy for colds and fevers—or for warding off such ills—in New England a century ago. Modern doctors, however, order other treatment.

Aside from such disputed medical matters, the flower cluster of the Boneset plant is not particularly handsome but it does decorate the meadows and roadsides late in the season when many of the more beautiful and more delicate flowers have faded from the scene. It is another member of the Composite Family, but, unlike the Daisy and many others in that great group that are composed of "ray flowers" and "disk flowers," its little flower heads that make up the big cluster are composed only of tiny tubular "disk flowers." It's a small matter to the naked eye but it will loom larger under a magnifying glass, and the beginner who looks into such things will be making real progress.

WHITE SNAKEROOT
(*Eupatorium rugosum*)

This is a first cousin of the Boneset, ranges over approximately the same territory, grows to about the same height, bears somewhat similar clusters of white flower heads, and is much like the Boneset in many botanical details, yet it is easy for even a beginner in the field to tell them apart. In the first place, look at the leaves! They are notably different from the odd-shaped joined leaves of the Boneset through which the stem pushes its way upward. These are heart-shaped and held away from the stem by a stalk or petiole from ½ to 2½ inches long. The floral spray of the Boneset is flat-topped and rather compact in appearance, with the flower heads so close together that the general effect is fuzzy. The floral spray of the White Snakeroot is more open by far and rounded or even scattering. The flower heads are not lost sight of in the mass but stand out like little round white buttons that you might think you could count without touching. Aside from these differences easy to note, Boneset prefers to lift its head to the open sky for the most part, whereas White Snakeroot is largely a dweller in the woods or at least in shady places. It is a very hardy flower, and, though it may come into bloom in July, it will linger late in Autumn and is one of the last of the flowers to succumb before the onslaught of frosty October nights or the cold rains of November. Just as the first flowers of Spring are sought with special fervor, the last flowers of the year are looked upon with extra affection. By then most of the trees are bare along the hillsides. The migrating Whitethroat Sparrows are scratching for food among the dead leaves of the thickets. "The melancholy days have come, the saddest of the year." It's then that the White Snakeroot, still in sturdy bloom, gladdens the eye and cheers the heart.

Like all members of the *Eupatorium* group of the Composite Family, it has flower heads composed entirely of "disk flowers," and in this case they put on a good show in a small way. But here again you really need a magnifying glass to appreciate it. The name "Snakeroot," of course, comes from a belief of old days that an infusion made from the root of the plant was a cure for the ill effects of a bite by a poisonous snake. Every region where poisonous snakes are found has at least one "Snakeroot" and probably several at the very least. Names to the same effect are found in many languages on different continents. But the belief in modern medical circles is that there are better ways of treating the ill effects of bites by poisonous snakes than by drinking down an infusion made from any part of any one of these plants—or all of them put together.

[71]

JOE-PYE WEED; PURPLE BONESET
(*Eupatorium purpureum*)

When the wine-colored sprays of the Joe-Pye Weed begin to appear in rich woods, along the roadsides, in wet meadows, and almost anywhere in moist ground over most of temperate North America, Summer is on the wane and Autumn is just around the corner. The common name "Joe-Pye Weed" covers at least four species of *Eupatorium* that range practically from coast to coast, but they look much alike to the ordinary eye and the specific differences are details that the beginner can set aside until he becomes well acquainted with the group. The species shown here is common in rich woods, in thickets, and along shady roadsides over the eastern half of the United States and nearby Canada and grows to a height of from 4 to 8 feet on a stem as stiff and as straight as a lance. The leaves that grow in "whorls" or circles of 3's to 6's around the stem like spokes of a wheel are about 6 inches long, narrowly oval, pointed at both ends, and sharply toothed along the edges. The stem often carries a purplish tint and usually is dark purple at the "nodes" or where the leaf "whorls" branch out from it. The large rounded floral sprays at the tops of the stems vary in color from a wishy-washy white through a weak pink and on into a light lilac or pale purple, depending upon the particular plant, the place in which it is growing, and

possibly local weather conditions. If you examine the floral sprays, you will find them made up of many little flower heads that are, in turn, gatherings of "disk flowers" according to the rule for the *Eupatorium* group. If this particular species prefers shaded territory, there are other Joe-Pye Weeds that prefer swamps, wet meadows, and river banks where they often provide a delicately tinted foreground for a picturesque landscape beyond. A hillside of Goldenrod above a swale of Joe-Pye Weed is truly a lovely combination of colors.

The Joe Pye after whom these flowers were named is supposed to have been an Indian medicine man who became friendly with the early colonists of Massachusetts and cured varied ills—typhus has been mentioned—by his skillful use of these plants. His medical secrets are now lost in a mist of legend, but Joe Pye himself, through the growing power of these tall plants, has achieved immortality of a kind, for his name will be preserved down the centuries as the great sprays of the Joe-Pye Weeds come annually into softly tinted bloom.

IRONWEED
(*Vernonia noveboracensis*)

This is still another member of the great Composite Family. As Wamba, the son of Witless, the son of an alderman, said—according to Sir Walter Scott in "Ivanhoe," though Wamba was speaking of another matter at the time: "Nomen est legio," meaning "Their name is legion" with Latin emphasis. So it is with the members of the Composite Family, and certainly the Ironweed can't be overlooked, because it is one of the tallest of the lot. When the Joe-Pye Weed is coming into bloom in low moist ground such as wet meadows, the fringes of brooks or streams, or the soggy borders of swamps, among those tall stalks bearing pinkish-purple sprays you may see here and there an even taller stalk carrying a wide floral spray of deep purple hue. That will be the Ironweed. There are half a dozen species of Ironweed fairly well distributed across the United States and southern Canada. They differ somewhat in size and flower color and in the shape of the leaves, but they look much alike to the ordinary observer and all of them are easily distinguished from the Joe-Pye Weeds—close relatives, by the way—among whom they often grow. The much deeper purple of the Ironweed flower spray is an easy guide because it stands out among the paler

Joe-Pye Weed blooms. Another striking difference is in the way the leaves grow out of the stems. The leaves of the Joe-Pye Weeds are "whorled" or set in circles at intervals along the stem, whereas the leaves of the Ironweed are individualists. They come as they please and only rarely or accidentally grow opposite one another on the stem. In fact, they seem to grow out at all angles, but each one usually starts at an otherwise unoccupied point along the stem. A glance at the picture will make this plain.

The New York Ironweed, as this particular species is named, is common in moist open or moderately shaded ground in the Northeast and extends as far south as Georgia and as far west as Mississippi. It grows from 3 to 9 feet high and comes into full bloom in August and September, but in favored locations it lingers in bloom into October. At a distance it might be mistaken for one of the tall purple Asters in September, but, on a nearer view, the difference is quite plain because the Ironweed has only tubular "disk flowers" where the Asters have a center of tiny "disk flowers" surrounded by a colorful circle of flat "ray flowers."

[73]

NEW ENGLAND ASTER

(*Aster novae-angliae*)

The Asters are a wonderful group; sturdy, widespread, beautiful, and abundant almost everywhere in uncultivated ground. Botanists have found some 200 species in North America. They are members of the Composite Family along with the Joe-Pye Weed and the Ironweed, but, with their centers of tightly packed tiny "disk flowers" and their radiating fringes of colorful strap-shaped "ray flowers," they bear a much greater resemblance to such other members of that almost overwhelming family as the Fleabanes, the Black-eyed Susan, and the Common White Daisy. Most of the Asters come into bloom rather late in the season, flowering in Autumn days and displaying "ray flowers" of all hues from pure white to deep purple. There are white Asters that cover the shaded floors of the September woods. There are Asters of many different tints to brighten the country roadsides in harvest time. The hunter finds them in the swamps and on brilliant October hillsides when he is out with dog and gun. The early migrants among the birds go southward over a landscape that is sprinkled with a hundred kinds of Asters beneath them. Do not worry about trying to identify all the Asters in your area. They are far too many in number, and not only are the specific differences small in many cases but the species interbreed on occasions and cause confusion even among licensed botanists. It is enough for a beginner to know a few species and love the whole family. A general rule for recognition is: if it looks like a Daisy, it is an Aster or some close relative of that group. This diagnosis will do until a botanist comes along to settle the matter.

The New England Aster is one of the tallest and most beautiful of the apparently endless kinds of Asters found over most of the United States and southern Canada. It grows almost everywhere in waste open territory and along roadsides, but it seems to prefer moist ground and the fringes of swamps or water courses of any kind. It has a stout and hairy main stem that sometimes reaches a height of 8 feet, though about 5 feet would be closer to the average. The narrow, hairy leaves are from 2 to 5 inches long and are alternate —not opposite one another—along the stem. They have no stalks or "petioles" and appear to "sit on" the stem in a manner the botanists call "clasping." Near the top the stem sends out many branchlets in a spreading spray and the lovely flower heads with golden centers and rich purple rays are carried at the ends of the branchlets. Over their full range they bloom from August into October, and where they grow amid patches of Goldenrod the color contrast is spectacular.

BROAD-LEAF GOLDEN ASTER
(*Chrysopsis mariana*)

The Golden Asters—there are more than a dozen species in North America—look much like yellow Daisies, and, depending upon the species and local conditions, they grow from a height of a few inches to about 3 feet. The Broad-leaf or Maryland Golden Aster reaches a height of 2½ feet, has a flower head about 1 inch across, and is plentiful in sandy soil and open woods from New York to Florida and westward to Ohio and Texas Most of the Golden Asters bloom from July to October, but the Broad-leaf usually waits until August to open its floral display. The golden-yellow flower heads are held up sturdily in a loose cluster (a "corymb") at the top of the stem, and where they grow in the New York and New Jersey seashore areas, they come into their golden prime about the time that the Summer vacationists are packing up to leave the beach and return to the city. If you roam the moors of Nantucket in August or September, you will find a different species of Golden Aster—the smaller, lower-growing, and narrow-leaved *Chrysopsis falcata* —brightening the footpaths and the fringes of the sandy rutted roads of that colorful region.

BRISTLY or STIFF-LEAVED ASTER
(*Aster linariifolius*)

This particular flower deserves a medal if for no other reason than that it is one member of the confusing Aster group that is easy to identify. It may be found over the whole eastern half of the United States and as far west as Minnesota and Texas, pushing up its "stiffy and starchy" stalks to a height of from 6 inches to 2 feet. The narrow leaves, 1 to 1½ inches long and shaped like blades of grass, are really stiff and rough to the touch. The flowers are easy to gather for a bouquet because they appear in patches and each stem usually carries from 2 to 5 or 6 flower heads at the top, though not all of them open at the same time. Though the Bristly Aster is widespread, it is often quite local in distribution. You may find a whole field covered with it—in dry soil on open hillsides or roadsides—and no other patches for miles around. Another odd point is that the patches often migrate in a body. They die out in one spot and move on to another. They come into bloom in August and may be found flowering to October. The "ray flowers" may be lavender, pale blue, or almost white, and the yellow "disk flowers" turn red-bronze as they mature, a customary change with many of the Aster group.

[75]

CLOSED GENTIAN; BOTTLE GENTIAN
(*Gentiana andrewsii*)

This flower is easy to recognize but not so easy to find, and it is definitely difficult to come to any agreement on a common name for it. The scientific name remains soberly constant—the *andrewsii* is in honor of Henry C. Andrews, an English flower painter of about 150 years ago—but in different parts of its range or by different persons it may be called Closed Gentian, Blind Gentian, Bottle Gentian, Barrel Gentian, Fringe-tip Closed Gentian, or Closed Blue Gentian. Take your choice. There is no law covering the matter. The flowers really do look much like little narrow blue barrels fairly well sealed at each end. The stiff straight stem grows to a height of from 1 to 2½ feet with narrow fleshy leaves that "sit close" and come in pairs on opposite sides of the lower section of the stem. Near the top they are "whorled" or in a circle around the stem and provide what appears to be a green supporting bracket for the clusters of flowers 1 to 2 inches long that grow out of the "axils" or upper side of the leaf-joints. The plant prefers moist ground and is found—often in ditches or on wet roadside banks—over most of the eastern half of temperate North America from Quebec to Georgia. The flowers come into bloom from August into October and it requires the strength and persistence of the burly Bumblebee to force its way into the folded-over tip of the flower to gather pollen for food and, in the process, fertilize the flowers as it goes from one to another on its foraging trip. The Closed Gentian often escapes notice even where it is fairly common because it hides away in lush growths and the clusters of blue flowers do not catch the eye as they would if they were brighter in hue. So go slowly and look carefully if you want to find the Closed Gentian.

There are some two dozen species of Gentian in North America and many species in Europe and Asia. The group is named for King Gentius of Illyria, the country that Shakespeare chose as a setting for *Twelfth Night* and the region that we now known as Albania and Yugoslavia. Gentius is recorded in herbal history as the original discoverer of medicinal virtues in these plants. He reigned in the 2nd Century B.C. and came upon dire misfortune beyond the curative powers of any Gentian. His army was routed by the invading Roman legions in 168 B.C. and he and his family were led as captives in a triumphal march through the streets of Rome.

FRINGED GENTIAN
(*Gentiana crinita*)

Finis coronet opus! Let the end crown all and the last be the best! Here is a lovely flower that often carries its beautiful and delicately fringed petals into the frosted foreground of oncoming Winter. Blooming from late August into November, it ranges from Maine to Manitoba and from Georgia to Iowa, preferably in overgrown wet meadows where the turf is soft underfoot, where the Woodcock feed and the White-eyed Vireos nest, and where pushing young Willows, Alders, Viburnums, Panicled Dogweeds, and Gray Birches are eager to establish themselves. You may find it along brooks or the edges of swamps or even in roadside ditches, but do not look for it in meadows that have been mowed or on roadsides that have been trimmed with a scythe, for there it will have been cut down before its time if it springs up at all. It grows to a height of 2 to 3 feet, with the flowers carried much as candles are carried by a multibranched candelabrum. There is no need further to describe either the plant or the lovely tubular flowers of 4 fringed blue petals that are open to the Autumn skies. The petals alone are enough to catch the eye, gladden the heart, and identify the flower of which William Cullen Bryant wrote:

Thou blossom, bright with Autumn dew,
And colored with the heaven's own blue,
That openest when the quiet light
Succeeds the keen and frosty night;

Thou comest not when violets lean
O'er wandering brooks and springs unseen,
Or columbines, in purple dressed,
Nod o'er the ground-bird's hidden nest.

Thou waitest late, and com'st alone,
When woods are bare and birds are flown,
And frosts and shortening days portend
The aged Year is near his end.

Then doth thy sweet and quiet eye
Look through its fringes to the sky,
Blue—blue—as if that sky let fall
A flower from its cerulean wall.

I would that thus, when I shall see
The hour of death draw near to me,
Hope, blossoming within my heart,
May look to heaven as I depart.

FINIS.

[77]